ABOVE ALL ELSE,
Guard Your Heart

by Joan Joseph & Judy Jenkins

www.xulonpress.com

The authors dedicate this book, with deep gratitude and love...

...To Lynda Bryson, who not only consistently supported us with her prayers, but also lent generous financial backing to help make our dream of publishing this book a reality. Lynda has been a long-time friend, a faithful promoter of our travelling devotional CD's, and joyful believer in our vision to share the messages of hope and healing that God lays upon our hearts. Lynda, your encouragement all along the way has meant so much to us both – thank you!

...To Todd Jenkins, who was involved in the discussions of each and every chapter of this book as we were writing and editing, and who always eagerly shared his ideas and input, whether we were receptive to them – "or not!" Thank you, Todd!

...And to Katie Kendrick, for all of her hard work and dedication to help us bring our words to life. This endeavor was just a dream for so long, and thanks to her creativity, enthusiasm, and wiliness to give of her time and talents, she has been an invaluable help in seeing that we realize this dream. Her guidance has allowed us to step into a new phase of our lives! Thank you, Katie!

Table of Contents

Introduction

Proverbs 4:23 "Above all else, guard your heart, for it affects everything you do." (NLT)

As I was thinking about the role of my heart, I had to meditate on what that really looks like. So I went to the very definition of "role" — the dictionary defines a *role* as: how something is specifically fitted or used; why it exists. Effectively: its job, or purpose, or position. If our heart is truly the center of our being, then it must be the core of who we really are. Yet – I don't know about you – but my heart seems to rule me at times and it is not always leading me in the right direction. For instance, as a grandmother, my heart can definitely get in the way when it comes to wanting to bless my grandchildren. Even when the Lord is telling me "No," I override His voice and allow my heart to rule, which never turns out right. It's because what is tender to me will speak louder to me than the voice of our heavenly Father. So, this situation started me on a new journey – that is to discover what truly is in my heart.

If you do not have a solid foundation of knowing *who you are* and *who God is*, you'll never come to know His true peace, which is our greatest security system when it comes to guarding our heart. This peace is born out of prayer. It causes you to look to Him and trust Him for what you cannot see. It leads you to rely on the character of God.

God's Peace will then help us learn how to live fully in the purpose God has for us, and isn't that what we're aiming for?

So let's begin this journey together. If our heart is the center of our very being, then our emotions surely must be connected to it. Our spiritual "heart" is the emotional core of who we are. Emotions can bring forth a positive life of their own, or they can damage our being. The bible has much to say about the heart of a man. The study of the heart of Man is massive – and, yes, God knows all of our hearts. In
I King 8:39:

> **"Then hear in heaven your dwelling place and forgive and act and render to each whose heart you know, according to all his ways (for you, you only, know the hearts of all the children of mankind)."** (ESV)

x

But the questions I have to ask myself are:
Do I know my own heart? And, *Am I being honest
with myself about it?*
What is the true state of my heart?

We obviously need to learn all we can about the human heart, with the intention that doing so will help us come to know ourselves better and improve our heart health – spiritually, as well as bodily, for indeed these matters are inexorably linked! (*We'll explore that link in greater depth in the chapters to come!*) God so wants each of us to be honest and true to ourselves. This means: when you notice that certain problems are cyclically occurring in your life, **that** is a signal that you need to spend time taking a spiritual inventory, and begin to ask yourself **why**? It's easy to blame everyone around you, but that doesn't fix the real problem because the real problem is a ***heart issue***.

Chapter 1

The Role of Your Heart

When the Bible speaks of the human heart, it is speaking of our will, our emotions and our psychology, which encompasses the whole gamut of who we really are, at our core. The problem with me is being truthful with myself and asking, in earnest, "Will the real me please stand up?"

Ask yourself this: Without Christ at the center of our being, Can we really know our true selves?

I am created for a purpose and my journey in life is to find out what that is. That means we have to start with salvation. When we said "YES" to Jesus, what did we really say "yes" to? I know it has to start with our minds and then go to our hearts. Yet many are unable to allow that acceptance to make the transition from our head to our heart, because we reason with it, but in all actuality it is a heart issue. So, if you are struggling with the security of *knowing* that you are saved and believing that God wants your heart for himself, you must first come to know that this surrender is the foundation of your original union with Him. God didn't appeal to your *intellect*, alone; he asked for your *faith*. The Enemy despises your heart because it is with your heart that you **believe** *unto salvation and righteousness*. It is through *believing with your heart*, that the process begins. Finally, your faith graduates through life's experience into the confidence called knowing. We have an enemy though — called Satan — who wants to stop the process because he knows that when you and I put our *heart into it*, it can never be taken away — for that's when we transcend our ambivalent mind, and will never again doubt our salvation. The inability to fully trust in our salvation shouldn't **stop** our journey, it should be the **beginning** of a journey of learning how to bring our damaged emotions into alignment with God's purpose for our lives.

This is an ongoing journey that God unfolds *as we become equipped to handle it*. Personally, I cherish that quality of God's love, because he never gives us what we can't handle.

A page from Joan's journal...
How God Began to Heal My Broken Heart

For me, learning how to begin healing my damaged emotions is a journey I didn't set out on until I was 38 years old. I had already been married for a number of years, with three children, two of which were in high school. After my parents had divorced, I found myself taking on the job of helping to rear my younger sister who was, at this point married, herself, and had an eight-month-old baby girl–the three of them living with us in our home. What a mess that all was! My husband had a drinking problem, and making right decisions was not the business we were in! Looking back, I can see that we were a train wreck just waiting to happen. Three days before Christmas, on my youngest son's birthday, our 8-month-old precious little angel, who brought so much love and joy to our home, suddenly became very sick, and with a high fever. My sister and I rushed her to the hospital, and as I ran through the double doors of Mercy Hospital in a panic, screaming as loud as I could for someone to help us, our angel was dying in my arms. She had contracted meningitis and her fever had spiked to 108 degrees in a matter of minutes.

I'll never forget the feeling of leaving that hospital without our precious baby girl. As I got into my car, all alone in that hospital parking lot, I was trying very hard to remember what my problems were, just moments before that trip to the hospital. The amazing thing was, as I went over them in my mind, not a single one seemed important anymore. If I could just have that sweet baby girl back, nothing else would matter. I was devastated, as the older auntie, and the one "in charge" at home, I blamed myself for not knowing she was as sick as she turned out to be, and so the "blame game" began. Now, we also had to grapple with the uncertainty that my son may have contracted the disease as well — this was a nightmare that just wouldn't go away.

In the midst of all my pain and loss and feelings of desperation, I cried out to God, and He answered me, by sending people into my family's life that could help us get through the horrible days ahead. We did not attend a church at the time, so I called a friend (who I now know had been praying for us, without me even being aware), and her Pastor came over to speak with us. He was there for us with more love and grace than we had ever known. In the months that followed, we came to know the Lord as our savior and friend, and we turned to Jesus and said "Yes! We need you to come into our broken hearts and heal them." We also made precious new friendships with people in our new church and fellowship.

I think we are like most of God's children—we came to Him in a time of need, and the wonderful thing is that he is always there when we call, no matter our motivation for calling on Him!

And God will continue to turn our pain into joy. He has always been there for me, through every hard time in my life, since that day so many years ago. My biggest regret is that I waited so long to begin this journey with the Lord and to discover my purpose for living. Every one of us has dealt with things in our life that have damaged our hearts, but it is really our emotions that have been damaged. So it is our emotions that must get healed in order for us to go to the next level that God has in store for us on this journey. You see, staying stuck in the hurt will only hurt us further and damage us more, keeping us from growing in our walk with Jesus.

A page from Judy's journal...
Letting God in

We start by being truthful and honest with our feelings and realizing that the hurt can only be healed as we address if with the Father. I'll explain what I mean by that in this way... When you're a child, something traumatic may happen to you, where you are the innocent victim. That trauma opens the door for damaged emotions to seep into your heart. For instance: fear, insecurity, abandonment, lack of trust, and so many other damaging emotions can enter our hearts this way; once there, they affect the way we filter God's grace, unconditional love, and intimacy with Him throughout our walk together.

Think of making coffee — you have a filter, in which you place the ground beans to keep them from getting into the finished pot of coffee. After you have already run water through the grounds and had your coffee, running fresh water through those same grounds in the used filter will produce water that is discolored. Over and over again this will happen, because of what you're pouring the water through. In the same way, it is our job to recognize in ourselves when we have issues that have seeped into our emotional heart, through which we begin to filter every decision, every problem that arises, and every relationship. What we don't realize is that what comes out the other side of the filter of our damaged heart is distorted and false.

Like that fresh water, poured through the used coffee grounds, our result is going to be discolored and tainted. When we allow God to heal those damaged emotions, then truth flows through and we are able to see God as He truly is, in all of His grace and unconditional love. Now, when we get there, we are open to receiving what He has for us. When we operate in God's grace and love, this will allow peace to rule in our life.

When we lose our peace and become anxious and worried, we begin to make radical decisions that can open up doors for demonic attack and turmoil in our lives. This is when we become confused, and that allows the enemy to suggest threats of impending danger, which can leave you terrified and shaken, causing you to lose the guard over your heart that would otherwise preserve you in whatever storm you are going through. This then starts a downward spiral to fear and deception.

On that note...

I had dealt with fear many times, and really thought I had a handle on it, but when my husband wanted to retire, fear really gripped me. My prayer partner, Joan, heard that fear in my voice. She is a great partner because she calls me on things–and this one, she called me on! Of course, I'd like to say that I owned up to it right away–Ha! No, I had to get alone and really search my heart to find out why this was causing such a problem. God began to reveal to me that I had allowed The World to dictate to me what retirement should look like. See, the issue of my heart was fear. Fear of losing everything and going backwards, of feeling I was not moving or going forward.

Fear had caused me to look at my situation from The World's view and its perspective, following its example of retirement, and not looking to God and trusting Him for his promises for my future. I love that God shared with me that He would never take me backwards but always move me forward. That *took me to the Word and allowed God to make what was not straight, straight again. Now, here I am, one year later in my Promised Land and I realize that if my husband hadn't lost his job, I would not be in the center of His will right now. Praise God! I chose not to listen to my heart but I grabbed hold of God's hand and said, "Yes, I will go!"*

Jeremiah 17:9-10: "The human heart is most deceitful and desperately wicked. Who really knows how bad it is? But I know! I, the Lord, search all hearts and examine secret motives. I give all people their due rewards, according to what their actions deserve." *(NLV)*

Why is that, you might ask? God makes it clear why we sin — it's a matter of the heart. Our heart is inclined toward sin from the time we are born. It is easy to fall into the routine of forgetting and forsaking God. But we can still choose whether or not to continue in sin. We can yield to a specific temptation, or we can ask God to help us resist temptation when it comes. We have to be open to allow God to speak to us without allowing the filters of our heart to interfere, because in today's society, we are so programmed to be self-centered and self-absorbed.

Understanding the role of your heart helps you to recognize the tools our enemy uses on our heart to deceive us. Again, for clarity, we go to the dictionary definition of "deception." Webster's dictionary defines deception this way: "To mislead by giving a distorted impression of false sense of reality." In other words, to trick you. The Word says there will be an increase in deception and a tremendous potential for people to be deceived. We see this everywhere we look—it comes to us through media, television, and news. Deception will tap into your weakness. The subtle attempt of Satan has always been to undermine the authority of the word of God. Deception compromises Divine provision and protection. The enemy spirit comes to deceive you and me so that:

1. He can take your eyes away from the path of God
2. Lead you from God's will
3. Place you in bondage
4. Torment you to frustration
5. Keep you so busy you'll never have real time with your Father.

When our hearts are deceived, they will lead us into many troubles, and much chaos.

The strategy of deception:

1. Distort what God says by changing the emphasis
2. Bring into question God's motive—always the result of twisted meaning.
3. Introduce reason that ultimately leads you to question God's goodness and integrity.

Once this deception is carried out, it's easy for the enemy to turn you against God's authority. This is why our hearts must be changed, regenerated, and we must know **what** we are filtering our decisions through.

James 1:22 says "But be ye doers of the Word and not hearers only." (KJ)

Because if you're only *hearing* and not *doing* what we're instructed by God's Word to do, then you're deceiving yourself. Following God in obedience is better than sacrifice. Yet we would rather distort God's truth to bend in *our* direction than change ourselves and bend *the world* back to God's truth.

How many of you think there has been some deception in your life? Let's not forget, Satan led one-third of the angels astray from the very presence of God in Heaven! He even caused Eve to disobey in a perfect environment. After all,

Eve had never been abused by a husband, frustrated by the demands of parenthood, or mistreated by a boss. Yet she was still led astray. Consider, then, the challenge of what we face, here on Earth in our *imperfect* environment, filled with trials and stresses. The likelihood that we all have been deceived in some way, at one time or another, is almost guaranteed.

Our heart is described in the scriptures as, essentially, *our most authentic personhood*. It is the place wherein all decisions are originated, and yet we are told that our hearts will deceive us. For this reason, it is **vitally** important that our heart is connected to our spirit. We make very poor choices and decisions about our lives when we are *totally* led by our heart. It is the place of our feelings, emotions, desires, passions, deep understanding, and our will–the very center of who we are. In other words, "You **are** what your heart **is**."

Proverbs 23:7 "For as a man thinks in his heart, so is he." (NKJ)

Let not your heart be troubled,
Give your worries and cares to me.
I am your Heavenly Father
Who suffered and died for thee.
There are times throughout your earthly life
When you are filled with doubts and fear.
Always come to ME in prayer
And know that I am near.
The love I have for you, dear child,
Can never be bought or measured.
It's a gift I freely give to you,
It is my most precious treasure.
When sorrow or pain come your way,
And life seems to be unfair,
Let not your heart be troubled...
Just come to ME in prayer.

Poem by Shirley Hile Powell

Chapter 2

The Importance of Guarding Your Heart

God is really wanting to warn us, so that we can walk, victoriously, with him.

So let's dig in:

> **Proverbs 4:20-27): "Pay attention, my child, to what I say. Listen carefully, don't lose sight of my words and let them penetrate deep within your heart. For they bring life to those who find them, and healing to their whole body."** Now, take special note here: **"Guard your heart above all else, for it determines the course of your life. Avoid all perverse talk; stay away from corrupt speech. Look straight ahead,**

and fix your eyes on what lies before you. Mark out a straight path for your feet; stay on the safe path. Don't get sidetracked; keep your feet from following evil." (NLV)

Wow! That's a strong word! Yet how exciting it is to know that our Father loves us so much that he gives us this warning. He has said to his children, essentially, "If you don't guard your heart, you will be open to a lot of things that will come in and pervert it." God *wants* us to have a pure heart! It's just like when we were little children — you know, when our parents tell us not to play in the street, and they may even *yell* at us, "Don't play in the street!" At the time, we might not want to hear them say that, because it's *fun* to play in the street, but our parents say those things to us because they know better, and they are *guarding* us from danger. That's just the thing that God is doing now.

Most of us have already stepped into things because we have never learned how to guard our hearts. God is really saying, "You don't have to continue in that; you can change it! You can decide now to put a guard over your heart and not let those things happen again." Think about it like this: When we were young, in the 1950's and 60's, in most places in America, you didn't worry about your home getting burglarized. We could take off and leave our doors unlocked, and our windows open, and we were sure that it was safe to do so — until one day when our home *is* broken into and we're robbed — what should we do? We go out and get an alarm system and cameras; we do all kinds of things to prevent that from happening again! But we're a day late and a dollar short, because we've already been robbed. Now we are paying attention — locking our doors and windows, because we have experienced what it's like to be violated in that way.

Just the other day in the grocery store, as I was just walking around looking at the produce selection, a lady came up to me and said, "You shouldn't leave your purse in your cart unattended like that." That lady shared that someone had once stolen her purse from her shopping cart because she had done the same. This woman said, "I hope you're not offended that I've said something to you, but it scared me when I saw that you weren't guarding your purse." Of course I said, "Oh, thank you so much..." and told her I appreciated the advice. As I continued my shopping, I realized that I have never had the experience of someone stealing my purse from my unattended shopping cart. With the absence of personal experience, we often walk around with our guards down, and can become lackadaisical about our surroundings, making us vulnerable to dangers we aren't even aware of. You need not feel guilty when you realize you're living this way, it is only human — and that is why God knows that learning to properly guard your heart is vital to our health and our protection.

God is saying to you and me: "If you have the ability to do *one thing* with your day, do this — *watch over your heart.*" Just as your **physical** heart determines how and what your body can do, so you're **spiritual** heart guides what you can and will do, spiritually. I don't think we always realize the power of the enemy that is against us. This enemy wants to embitter and corrupt us and he does that through our heart. The enemy doesn't want us guarding against anything! He wants us open to contamination so he can come in and pollute us; so that everything that runs through our heart will come out wrong.

I've seen people live their whole life and never get past an injury or allow themselves to move forward from their past. It's true that *most* of us never have death with the pain and the problems of our past, and it has left an impression on our hearts. I think this is what God is talking about — he wants us to deal with our issues of lust, loneliness, rejection, abandonment, etc. God wants us to choose wisdom and not be ignorant or ignore our past, because when we do, we are not totally healthy. When there is pain (*and there **will** be pain that will come your way...!*) you have to address it; you must go after it; and you cannot just put that hurt away in a box and pretend like it will be contained there forever. You can be sure — it will *always* come back up!

Healing comes when you begin to know what God thinks about you, what God believes about you, and how He feels about you. He wants to be the very center of our being. He wants us to have His heart. We all have been a victim at one time or another in our lives – and **really** – Jesus knows what it means to be a victim. He was, himself, an innocent victim. God tells us not to allow that one incident, or those few times when you have suffered, to ruin the rest of the life He has planned for you. Get to *know* your heart, come to God and allow Him to enter it, and get to the *root of your problems*. God wants to do this work *with you* and *for you*. He is telling us "above all else," take a moment and realize that you need a security system over your heart. And that security system – if you choose to sign up for it! – is called Jesus Christ.

One problem we run into is that we tend to guard our hearts in the *wrong ways*. We put up a universal barrier, or a shield, and we think that by doing so, we can't get hurt ever again. However, *this* kind of barrier can stop our own healing before it's even begun. When we put up the wrong kind of shield, we block intimacy with God, and we might begin to see Him as the "judgmental Father," and not as a friend who has come to help and set us free. God wants to give us the spirit of discernment, so that the enemy cannot pollute us, destroy us, or bring us down. God wants to lift you up — out of the pit, out of your prison, and into his light! When you are lifted up in this way, you will begin to live in the light of His truth, so that you may know His peace, joy, rest, and purposes.

We have led enough counseling sessions in our lives to know that women who never dealt with abuse at a young age go on to live their Christian lives with a wounded heart. It will cause many problems as they get older, because each of us must learn that we **are** what our heart **is**. The very core of our being is our heart. This is the place where we make all decisions; it is the source of our feelings, our desires, our thoughts and our will — so if our heart is damaged, and if we're allowing things in that feed the problems and the pain, we will *never* get well. This will also keep us from being all that God created us to be.

A page from Judy's journal...
Filtering Through a Damaged Heart

*At a time in my life when needing to make a very important decision, I filtered that decision through **my heart**, and not through the wisdom of the **heart of my Father**. I had been asked to attend a meeting with my boss, who I had already said goodbye to when I left that place of business. I was asked to return, to meet with him, along with his supervisor, to further* *discuss things, as a way of achieving some closure, for them. Everything in me said "NO," and yet my own heart was saying that a true, loving Christian would go to that meeting and show them the light, and the true person I really am. Now, in my reasoning, that all sounded good and, yes, I was going to be the better person! But the real truth was that I was still trying to prove a point, from my wounded heart, and any decision I would make from it would not be Godly, but instead one of the flesh, because of what I was filtering it through. I'm talking about rejection, pride, and a feeling of being abandoned – not a good filter for any decision to be made from. The outcome of that meeting left me even more wounded because I followed my heart and not God's heart. The enemy knows just how to speak to us, and that makes such sense, but God calls us to be humble and obedient. No matter how you look, we all struggle with that.*

After that meeting with my former boss, I became depressed, withdrawn, and felt so alone. I became disappointed in God that day, and I even started to feel that God left me out to dry, that He wasn't even with me in that meeting. It wasn't until a year later, as I began to ask for forgiveness of being disappointed in God, and allowed the Father to put me back in alignment with His will, that God spoke to me so clearly, while I was journaling one day. I had asked him, "Father, remember that meeting I had, when I asked you to be with me, and guide me, and help me? I never understood why you didn't help me." He said so clearly to me, "Because, I never asked you to go to the meeting at all! Because I never required that of you." There was such a breaking in me, in that moment, and I cried out to God, asking again for forgiveness for listening to my heart that day and not the heart of my Father. I realized I had a heart that needed mending, and so the journey began! I started to look inward at my true problems, asking the Father each time to heal that section. I had to go back as far as my childhood, which allowed me to begin to see the pain and hurt I felt, which allowed me to put up an unhealthy guard around my heart. This was not a good guard, but it was a purely protective guard.

God was sharing with me, at that moment, that when your heart is damaged and you haven't dealt with the heart issues, then you will make a decision in your mind, which you will then run through the filter of your damaged heart. Any decision made that way doesn't come out clear and decisive; we don't see things from God's perspective in those times, because we have allowed our damaged heart to be a filter. When you do this, your decision-making ability is tainted, because you are filtering it through something that may have happened to you 20 years ago—or longer!—And you see things from a wrong perspective. The problem is, filtering decisions through the pain of the past, and attempting to do it on our own, we are never going to get a handle on things, because without the wisdom of God's heart, we don't know how to deal with our own wounded heart.

Proverbs 23:7a says, "For as he thinks in his heart, so is he." (NKJ) Also in, I Samuel 16:7 "For Man looks on the outward appearance, but God looks at the heart." (NKJV)

God is really interested in the condition of our heart he understands we have all these weaknesses. He wants us to have a pure heart, and as we read in

Jeremiah 17:9 "the heart is deceitful above all things and desperately wicked, who can know it." (KJV)

God is talking about the condition of our heart, and as I was reading and studying this lesson I realized that the *physical* conditions of our *physical* heart, are connected to our *spiritual* heart.

Here's a Biblical example: If Samson had guarded his heart, Delilah wouldn't have weakened him. Had Samson guarded his heart with the breastplate of righteousness that Paul talked about, he would have continued to be productive in Israel. But in the heat of his passion, and the weariness of his life, Samson "told her all the secrets of his heart" (**Judges 16:17**). What a tragedy! Samson's weakness caused him to pollute his heart with lust and loneliness, and he gave it to someone other than God. *There are some things you give to no one but God.*

Many of us have given our hearts to people, to careers, and to ideals–but remember, not all **good** ideas are **God** ideas. The "God idea" is conceived and nurtured in the womb of prayer. It is not a venture or an attempt. Its birth comes by simply acting out the plan God gives you through prayer.

Once you know you have a "God idea," refuse to allow anyone to intimidate you with earthly wisdom. When you have received God's counsel on an issue it *settles it*. Don't let the plans of the Lord be contaminated by well-wishers who may not have the mind of the Lord for that particular situation. Don't be confused by the manipulation of others. Some people are so indecisive that they are difficult to follow. Those who never make definite decisions allow the enemy to shift God's agenda right out of their lives!

Know this–God wants your heart for Himself.

Amos 7:7-8: "Then He showed me another vision, I saw the Lord standing beside a wall that had been built using a plumb line. I

answered 'A plumb line.' And the Lord replied, 'I will test my people with this plumb line. I will no longer ignore all their sins.'" (NLV)

A plumb line is a device used to ensure the straightness of a wall. A wall that is not straight will eventually collapse. God wants His people to be right with Him. He wants the sin that makes us crooked removed immediately. God's word is the plumb line that helps us become aware of our sins.

Think about this... How do you measure up to God's plumb line?

"Be careful for nothing; but in everything by prayer and supplication with thanksgiving let your requests be made known unto God. And the peace of God, which passes all under- standing, shall keep your hearts and minds through Christ Jesus" (Philippians 4:6-7) (KJV)

Here, the word 'keep' is better translated as 'guard.' God's peace will guard your heart and mind. It will cause you to pick out what thoughts you will entertain. Samson entertained Delilah, and she infiltrated his heart and took his secrets. Avoid entertaining thoughts that will destroy your peace.

Whenever I catch myself rehearsing problems over and over, I know I am entertaining those problems. They will "cut my hair of anointing" if I don't abort them! How can a thought be "aborted"? Whatever you give *attention* to, you give *power* to. Let me explain. Say I'm speaking to a group of people and I have a person in that setting that is disrupting me in the meeting, by drawing attention to themselves. If I stop the meeting and call that person out by name, then I have just shifted the power over to that person (the enemy) and allowed them to abort what God wanted to do in the meeting. When my thoughts continually want to focus on my problem and situation, I weaken myself from receiving the power and strength God wants to give to me, which will help me become an overcomer.

When our thoughts keep going back to nursing, cursing, and rehearsing our problems, we have to line up our soul with our spirit. Which means we need to use the tools God has given us to overcome, by reining in our thoughts, for instance: putting on some praise music or quoting a scripture out loud, because the mind can't do **both** that **and** focus on the problems you've been running over and over in your heart and mind. A good scripture to quote is:

Philippians 4:8-9 "Summing it all up, friends, I'd say you'll do best by filling your minds and meditating on things true, noble, reputable,

authentic, compelling, gracious—the best, not the worst; the beautiful, not the ugly; things to praise, not things to curse. Put into practice what you learned from me, what you heard and saw and realized. Do that, and God, who makes everything work together, will work you into his most excellent harmonies." (MSG)

If life has dealt you some tough cards, don't give up. You may be down, but bless God you are not out! Strengthen the things that remain and go on. You will never survive the challenges of life if you make decisions without God's guidance. God wants to teach you the significance and power of daily communion with Him. It's The Word that gives us strength, so we need to **ask** the Lord to show us which scriptures are for us in the season we are in. It is the Word that empowers us to overcome. The Word brings life to a dead situation, and hope to a hopeless heart.

You are in the ring with a formidable opponent, who wants to take you out right now! Your enemy knows that God has pre-destined you for greatness. He would love to destroy you with a single blow. But he doesn't have the power to take you out if you have a Guard over your heart. The problem is, when we live without guarding our heart, or without concern for protection from the enemy, we open the door to a hard heart and an unbelieving, proud heart; an unclean heart, which makes us insensitive to God's leading. That is why God say's with all diligence Guard your heart. It is an action not to be ignored. To be successful, you must set your mind to it with great conviction, making you aware: ***above all else guard your heart***.

Today, make a commitment to stand in God's strength, regardless of the challenges or questions life brings and regardless of how hard you are hit. You may feel the sting of the devil's blows, and you may even feel the pain, but give him a clear message with a determination:

"I will not quiet. I will not stop serving my Lord, and I Will not lean on my own understanding."

That is why the heart is to be watched closely — because there is great danger that it will be turned away. We often don't even realize that *every day* we are influenced by many seductive forces. If we allow it, these can–and eventually will–destroy us. Sometimes, despite all that we do, challenging situations still arise; but it is foolish not to take every precaution to make it as difficult as possible for a thief to break in. The enemy comes to kill, steal and destroy. Why do we think He won't be after us? Because the enemy has deceived us into believing we are not important enough in God's plans for this life, and that is a lie from the Pit of Hell. God has a plan for each and every one of us and has a purpose for our lives. We are all vitally important to the bigger picture that God has for our lives. We have to grab hold of this and that is why God says, "**Above all else guard your heart.**"

Many men are ready to defend their families from physical assailants, but few men are prepared to defend their families against spiritual attacks. Although they have fought off thieves and criminals, they are still plagued by inner guilt, private perversion, and moral problems. They are poorly equipped to build defenses against depression, suicide, child abuse, or other spirits that may target their home. We can't kill these things with guns, but we can stop them cold with prayer!

Think about this... How are you praying?

The Devil hates to see a husband and wife praying together, in agreement prayer, because they become a cord unbroken as they partner with Jesus. They invite the power of God to guard their homes through intercession. As a praying mother and a grandmother I have learned the power of standing in the position of authority over my children and grandchildren. When we cover our family with prayer, God's protection is released on them. We need to realize we have been given the incredible gift and responsibility to use the tools given to us to protect this next generation, we come to the battle with unstoppable force and unbeatable weapons.

Stand guard over your loved ones with prayer. Let your children see you ministering through prayer. Prayer is a mighty tool to protect those you love. When you pray, God often gives direction and instruction to help you safeguard your family from attack. He did it for Noah, and for Joseph and Mary, and He will do it for you.

> **"If you want to know what God wants you to do, ask him, and he will gladly tell you, for he is always ready to give a bountiful supply of wisdom to all who ask him; he will not resent it. But when you ask him, be sure that you really expect him to tell you, for a doubtful mind will be as unsettled as a wave of the sea that is driven and tossed by the wind; and every decision you then make will be uncertain, as you turn first this way and then that. If you don't ask with faith, don't expect the Lord to give you any solid answer" (James 1:5-7).** (TLB)

Think about this...

*Do you have a spiritual heritage? Are there any miracles in your life? Are there any things you **know** God did for you?*

Guard this heritage of God's faithfulness, and preserve it, by passing it on to your sons and daughters. It may save them from needless mistakes and sorrow. They will know what you know without having to suffer what you suffered!

Why is this so important? Because God blesses you according to what is in your heart. If you are being kind, giving, loving and sharing *because it is in your heart* and you are not looking for anything in return, then that is a heart that God wants to bless. If you change who you are because you've been hurt, then you've changed the thing that God wants to bless you according to, and that is your heart. The people who hurt you are not worth that. You can lose everything that you have, but don't let anybody change your heart.

Three reasons why this is absolutely vital:

1. **Because your heart is extremely valuable**. We don't guard worthless things. I take my garbage to the street every Wednesday night, to be picked up on Thursday morning. It sits on the sidewalk all night, completely unguarded. Why? Because it is worthless and doesn't need to be guarded.

2. **Because your heart is the source of everything you do**. King Solomon says it is the "wellspring of life." In other words, it is the source of everything else in your

Above All Else, Guard Your Heart

life. Your heart overflows into your thoughts and into your words and especially into your actions.

3. **Because your heart is under constant attack**. When Solomon says to 'guard your heart," he implies that you are living in a combat zone — one in which there are going to be casualties.

On that note...

Satan uses all kinds of weapons to attack our heart. For me, these attacks often come in the form of some circumstance that leads to disappointment, discouragement, or even disillusionment. In these situations, I am tempted to quit—to walk off the field and surrender.

Did you know?

... An unguarded heart can open the door
to physical problems as well?

Heart murmurs are abnormal flow patterns due to faulty heart valves. Heart valves act as doors to prevent backward flow of blood into the heart. *Spiritual* heart murmurs occur when believers engage in complaining, gossip, disputes, and contention. Believers are instructed many times to avoid grumbling, murmuring, and complaining (**Exodus 16:3; John 6:43; Philippians 2:14**). By engaging in these activities, believers shift their focus away from the plans, purposes, and past blessings of God to the things of the world. God sees this as a lack of faith, and without faith, it is impossible to please God (**Hebrews 11:6**). Instead, Christians are instructed to strive for contentment in all things, trusting in God to provide what is needed in His good time. Guarding against an ungrateful spirit and cultivating a true sense of gratitude and trust is an important step toward guarding the heart.

> **"If then there is any encouragement in Christ, if any consolation of love, if any fellowship with the Spirit, if any affection and fulfill my joy by thinking the same way, having the same love, sharing the same feelings, focusing on one goal. Do nothing out of rivalry or conceit, but in humility consider others as more important than yourselves. Everyone should look out not only for his own interests, but also for the interests of others." (Philippians 2:1-4)** (HCSB)

Congestive heart failure

From Gerald Flury

Congestive heart failure is an inability of the heart to successfully pump blood through the body due to weaknesses within its walls. Congestive heart failure can result from hypertension (high blood pressure), myocardial infarctions (heart attacks), and abnormal enlargement of the heart. The *spiritual equivalents* are anger, giving in to temptation, and pride. Of all of the deadly sins, anger can be the hardest one to avoid. Anger acts like a poison on the body, both physically and spiritually, and makes a believer more vulnerable to the temptation to hurt others with our actions and words.

A page from Joan's journal...
Letting Go of Anger

*At one time, anger was a huge stronghold in my life, and it controlled me for many years. I used to think that my anger problem was due to **other** people **making** me angry. It seemed as though they would just come out of the woodwork, looking for me! Even things like, when I was driving the car, someone would flip me off or yell at me, and in my everyday life I seemed to always run into people with an attitude, or a chip on their shoulder – and I would take them on! It was causing me so much pain and trouble in my life, and I just couldn't see why everyone had it out for me.*

After I became a Christian, and started doing some real soul searching, I ended up seeing a counselor. She picked up on my anger issues, and she once made a statement that *changed my life forever: she said, "If **anyone** can make you angry about **anything**, then **you** are the one with the problem." Well, needless to say, I left there angry at her, feeling like she was making it all my fault. So, I went home and prayed about it and I knew in my heart that she was right. You see, I had a stronghold of anger that was rooted in deep hurt, and that anger had become my friend and a shield of protection. From within my stronghold of anger, I felt that if I could stay in control of my life, no one could ever hurt me again! At that point, my journey to healing began, and I have to tell you – those people who used to make me so angry, suddenly went away. I can't really remember the last time I got angry about anything! Oh, I have gotten upset about something, like all of us do from time to time, but I get over it quickly. Those of us who deal with anger as a stronghold know that feeling of anger that can easily turn into rage, and then you find yourself saying and doing the most terrible things; you just hate yourself afterward.*

I encourage you to stop this terrible cycle, let God heal all that pain and hurt in your heart, and get well physically, emotionally, and spiritually.

Ephesians 4:31-32 instructs, "Get rid of all bitterness, rage and anger, brawling and

slander, along with every form of malice. Be kind and compassionate to one another, forgiving each other, just as in Christ God forgave you." *(NIV)*

Congestive heart failure can be brought on by lethargy, feelings of purposelessness, a lack of goals or drive. Like with heart failure, many organs don't receive enough oxygen and nutrients, which damages them and reduces their ability to function properly.

Ephesians 4:16 "From whom the whole body, being fitted and held together by what every joint supplies, according to the proper working of each individual part causes the growth of the body for the building up of itself in love."(NASB)

Heart Blockage: Stubbornness and Resistance to Holy Spirit

From Pastor Jerry Flury

Psalms 81: 11-12 "But my people would not listen to me; Israel would not submit to me,

so I gave them over to their suborn hearts to follow their own devices."(NIV)

Enlarged Heart: Inflated Egos; Pride
From Pastor Jerry Flury

Proverbs 28:25 He who is of a proud heart stirs up strife, but he who trusts in the Lord will be prospered."(KJV)

Proverbs 16:18 Pride goes before destruc-tion, and a haughty spirit before a fall.*"(NIV)*

Here's an example: A minister, a Boy Scout, and a computer expert were the only passengers on a small plane. The pilot came back to the cabin and said that the plane was going down but there were only three parachutes and four people. The pilot added, "I should have one of the parachutes because I have a wife and three small children." So he took one and jumped. The computer whiz said, "I should have one of the parachutes because I am the smartest man in the world and everyone needs me." So he took one and jumped. The minister turned to the Boy Scout and with a sad smile said, "You are young and I have lived a rich life, so you take the remaining parachute, and I'll go down with the plane." The Boy Scout said, "Relax, Reverend, the smartest man in the world just picked up my knapsack and jumped out!"

Proverbs 16:5, says, "Everyone proud in heart is an abomination to the Lord" (NIV)

Pride was the first great sin of Satan, when he thought that he could be like God and incited one-third of the angels to leave and go with him. For this reason, Satan was cast from heaven. Satan also tempted Eve in the Garden of Eden by appealing to her ego. He appealed to Eve's ego and pride as he suggested she become as wise as God, so she capitulated to Satan's advice to eat of the fruit of the tree. Pride was, therefore, the downfall of man, as well. Satan did not want man to obey God but to become his own god—determining for himself reality, meaning and ethics.

How do I get an undivided heart in practical ways? Your daily intent and decision must center on getting time before God in the Word and prayer and asking God to become the focus of the mind, emotions, and heart.

Truth must rule. Significant spiritual warfare will need to occur at this point. To "guard your heart" means *knowing* and *believing* the truth of the Word, claiming God's promises, standing on His Truth, and standing your ground on that truth. An undivided heart means that the heart becomes your servant rather than the other way around. Let God and His Word, through the Holy Spirit, have control today. Do whatever it takes. Begin now protecting the most complex and vital and far-reaching part of you.

And now, we pray...

Father, I thank you for creating within me a wise and discerning heart, so that I am able to distinguish between right and wrong. Father, I trust in you with all my heart and lean not on my own understanding; in all my ways, I acknowledge you, and you will make my paths straight. Through your precepts, I get understanding; therefore I hate every false way. Your Word is a lamp to my feet, and a light to my path.

I make (special) request, (asking) that I may be filled with the full (deep and clear) knowledge of your will in all spiritual wisdom and in understanding and discernment of spiritual things—that I may walk (live and conduct myself) in a manner worthy of you, Lord, fully pleasing to you and desiring to please you in all things, steadily growing and increasing in and by your knowledge (with fuller, deeper, and clearer insight, acquaintance and recognition).

- From "Prayers That Avail Much" from Germaine Copeland

Chapter 3

Iniquities of the Heart

What are iniquities? This is not something we are often taught, or hear a lot about in church. The meaning of iniquities is: gross injustice, and immoral sins. Or another translation is: An unjust act or absence of moral or spiritual values.

Why is it important to know about iniquities?

The Hebrew meaning is: perverseness, bowed down, twisted, to be bent or crooked. Iniquity will eventually lead us to sin, and many times will keep you from your destiny. Iniquity is the same as *ungodliness*. Any area of our life that is not set apart for God is an iniquity. The way we take possession of the garden of our heart is to be cleansed of all our iniquities. We're talking about a deep-seated attitude hidden in our heart that lies quietly there but wants to rule over us. It is that thing in us which we fight against; which we *know* is wrong; and which we recognize so often in *other people*, and detest it.

The word iniquity in Hebrew is used to express how a human heart is not holy – not set apart – not Godly.

Psalms 58:3, even from birth the wicked go astray; from the womb they are wayward and speak lies. (KJV)

Their corrupt ways are not sporadic; they act in accordance with their nature, like in

Psalms 51:5, surely I was sinful at birth, sinful from the time my mother conceived me. Surely you desire truth in the inner parts; you teach me wisdom in the inmost place. (NKJV)

We're talking about generational strongholds, passed down from generation to generation. This is why we must *not* ignore, but *always* address, and allow the Lord to pull these deep-ly-held things out from our hearts, in order for wholeness to rule. We must not be deceived about ourselves; we must *want the truth* because it is the truth within us that sets us free.

What is the difference between iniquity and sin?

Some people think that sin and iniquity are the same thing.

Yet, in Isaiah 59:2, "but your iniquities have separated you from God; your sins have hidden his face from you so that he will not hear." (NKJV)

To understand further, we must know this: there are three different aspects of the whole fallen nature of man.

- **Iniquity = Perversion**. It is a gross immorality of injustice and wickedness. The Hebrew meaning is: perverseness, bowed down, twisted; to be bent or crooked; to be wrong; out of course. The word "iniquity" is used to express how a human heart is not holy – not set apart, not perfect, not godly.
- **Transgression = Rebellion**. Talking about a violation of the law, command, or duty: The exceeding of due bonds or limits. Rebellion against the path of Godly living. The Hebrew meaning of transgression is a willful deviation from, and therefore rebellion against, the path of godly living. The Greek meaning of transgression is: To go beyond; Overstepping the limits. This word very strongly

links with rebellion and disobedience. Transgressions are more potent than just sinning and are the next step into further permanent bondage. Transgressions are related to the word "trespass," which is a willful violation of the law.

- **Sin = Missing the mark**. Insufficient to satisfy a requirement or meet a need resulting from such inadequacy. The English word for Sin is derived from archery, hence, "missing the mark." The Hebrew meaning of sin is: Slipping away from where you should be. Sin refers to an action, something that happens in the real world, in real time.

Like in Proverbs 25:28, whoever has no rule over his spirit is like a city, broken down, without walls. (NKJV)

Bottom line: Iniquity is an attitude of the heart!

On that note…

When a person is living with an iniquity of the heart, there is a deep sadness that accompanies it. Often times one can't even name what that sadness is, where its roots are, or why they seem to feel an underlying sense of dis-ease beneath an otherwise "happy" life. Left un-checked, the iniquity can allow a terrible and dangerous separation between thoughts and actions; between knowledge of what we **should** be doing, and what we will allow ourselves to act upon. In other words, the iniquity can so strongly influence our actions that we will disregard the good and righteous things we have every reason in the world to live for. An un-checked iniquity of the heart is what allows us to self-sabotage – and don't we all know something about that, in one form or another? Whether it's living a double-life, experiencing a split-personality, delving into unspeakable sin while maintaining a façade of holiness – these very serious actions are made manifest in so many lives because of an iniquity of the heart that poisons anything good they may have gained otherwise. The insidious nature of iniquity can only be healed when we face it head-on – as painful as it may be. The most shameful secrets of our hearts have got to be brought to light in order for us to get our power back, and to live a life that is fully in agreement with the will of our Father.

God wants to change our lives and bring us to a season of fruitfulness in all areas. Now, fruitfulness is the *will of God* for us *individually and as a Church*. God wants us to become like the Garden of Eden. The way to achieve this is by getting rid of our iniquities. This is the great secret that shows the difference between a **true relationship** with God and just a **religious experience**.

Think of iniquity as the same as ungodliness, or being unholy. Any area of our life that is *not set apart for God* is an area of iniquity. God accepts you just as you are. He loves you even if you have iniquities, but he cannot bless you if you have wrong attitudes that burst from your heart.

> **James 1:23-25 says; "For if a man is a hearer of the word and not a doer, he is like a man that looks intently at himself in the mirror, for he looks at himself and goes away and at once forgets what he was like. But the one who looks at the perfect law, the law of liberty, and perseveres, being no hearer who forgets but a doer who acts, he will be blessed in his doing." (NKJV)**

A person that has a *religious* spirit, and a spirit of pride, thinks that he is already purified from His iniquities because he doesn't commit sin very often. However, God has a higher plan, he wants to bless you by removing the iniquities out of your life. For we all sin and come short of the glory of God. There is no sinless person on this earth. We're talking about *justifying* that one area in your life where you think *"I really have it all together; I'm pretty good."*

A man of *words*, but not *deeds*, is like a garden full of weeds.

Isaiah 59:2 says, "But your iniquities have separated you from God; your sins have hidden his face from you so that he will not hear." Matthew 24-12 says, "And because iniquity shall abound, the love of man shall wax cold." (KJV)

After an array of failures and sins, people get tired, and instead of just dumping the traditions of men, they dump everything and consider all things lawful for they are under grace. They lose their discernment in the thrill of finding liberty and end up on the other extreme, justifying things that appeal to the flesh, without considering that they may cause others to stumble and be condemned by the things they allow. They may even use love to manipulate other believers, or get others to do things that they have no faith to do, making them sin and ultimately stumble. They push the idea under the banner of grace. That's because we are so good at faking things. *Our enemy has a counterfeit for everything God has that is real.* Part of our process of growing is dying to ourselves so that Christ can become more alive in us and, we can become less. In this process is where we must look at everything in our heart, and our motives for what we think, and why we respond the way we do and react to things around us.

Many people do not want to deal with all of that – they are very happy just faking it, and brushing it off as *"It's the way I'm wired,"* or *"Just the way I was made."* My question to those who don't care to get deeper than that is this: *Is it, really, 'just the way you are?' How do you know?*

This kind of conversations we sometimes have within our-selves is called **deception**, and it is Satan's best weapon against mankind. He used this weapon against Eve, in the garden. It was so effective that he has continued to use it since. As long as The Church proclaims the truth of the gospel under the anointing of the Holy Spirit, his lies are revealed. Those who do *not* believe the gospel as the truth are trapped with Satan's lies. His lies are rapidly covering the world with darkness. And sadly, God's chil-dren are His greatest followers — believing that God's Grace approves. *What a lie that is!*

John 3-19 says "And this is the condemna-tion that light is come into the world, and men love darkness rather than light, because their deeds are evil. Jesus is the light of the world and those who walk with him do not walk in darkness."(KJV)

When we do not accept the truth, then we must accept a lie. God will send a strong delusion on them because they have despised the truth.

I fully acknowledge: sometimes the truth seems unbearable to face. For this reason, so many people readily accept something a bit more compatible, and comfortable, for themselves. If it seems to promise them everlasting life, without any major changes in their lifestyle, they will accept it without *really* searching it out. Christ came to rescue us and not enable us, and with Salvation comes transformation. We are to be **transformed** from our former life of sin and rebellion, and to become everyday more like Christ. It is *popular* to be open-minded toward many types of sin, calling them "personal choices" or "alternative lifestyles." but when the body of believers begins to tolerate sin, it is dangerously lowering standards and compromising the witness of the gospel. This is how false doctrines come to be accepted — because they seem "suit us" much better — but a lie is a lie is a lie, and it cannot save you.

As human beings, we do not like to be forced to give up our pleasures, or to be forced out of our comfort zones. We must remember we said "Yes!" to Jesus because we wanted something *more* — and that means we die for Christ to live in us. The Gospel challenges us and our preconceived ideas, which is what we refer to as our "flesh," or the very human element of pleasure-seeking, and comfort-making, as default response to the world.   If we *like* our sinful ways, we will *hate* those who try to convince us of our sins, and the need to repent and change our lifestyle. The gospel *is* good news, but it irritates the sin in us, and the hidden places in our hearts, often to the point that we are unwilling to let them go. Today in our churches, we hate to admit that we still are dealing with our sinful nature. We hesitate to go forward and fall on our knees in need of help from our savior — afraid that someone else may think we don't "have it all together."

As Christians, we need to recognize that we have sins in our lives, and we need to repent of them on a daily basis. God wants us to keep a short list of our wrongs, which includes our mind and our thinking.

A page from Judy's journal...
Understanding the Meaning of 'Iniquities'

I didn't fully understand the concept of iniquities until I began to take communion on a daily basis. It all started when I contracted MRSA and eventually had it six times – and the sixth time, it was literally killing me. So I ran to the Father and asked how to stop it. The doctors could do no more for me; I was desperate at this point. Crying out to God and asking for help, He laid on my heart the insistence to read a book about communion, which I of course read, called Eat my Flesh and Drink My Blood, *by Ana*

Mendez Ferrell. As God began to teach me about the power of communion, I began to partake. During my prayer time with my Prayer partner, as I was praying, I began to cry out for God to touch and heal the iniquities of my heart. I was surprised by what came out of my mouth because I didn't fully understand what that meant. But at that time God was working on the deep-rooted areas of my heart that I have kept closed up to him; places where I was unwilling to allow Him to enter. But as I began to confess my hurts, my anger, my disappointments, my lack of faith, my fears, and my lack of trust, God began to show me His grace, and healing began. Healing is a journey. We must come into agreement with Him that we need to be healed. I was ready to go all the way with God. I am happy to say that it has now been almost three years, and I have not had another bout of MRSA, and by God's grace, I never will.

God speaks to us very strongly about our iniquities, especially before his return to earth. It is Man's iniquities that will be his downfall during the end times. Many of God's children have never dealt with the issues deep within our hearts. It is what will pull on your heart during tough times and cause you to doubt, complain, and find fault with God – even walk away.

So how do we get cleansed from our iniquities?

The word says, in Ezekiel 36:37 "Thus says the Lord God: On the day that I cleanse you from all your iniquities…" (KJV)

This seems almost too simple to be true — *If we are cleansed from iniquities, the blessings will come?* I want that! Don't you? If you want to get rid of your iniquities, you need to be washed by the Word. God places Pastors, Evangelists, Teachers, Apostles and Prophets in your way so that you can identify the iniquities of your heart, act upon it, and move toward your healing!

And now, we pray...

Lord, reveal the steps that I should take to break what appears to be a generational curse. The sins of the fathers are being repeated in our household, and I do not want this curse passed down to my children. Father: Your Word says that we are over-comers by the blood of the Lamb and by the word of our testimony. Help me in the name of Jesus, I am committing my heart and my iniquities to you – I want to obey you and not my own desires. Show me the path of life for me and my family. Amen.

- From Prayers That Avail Much, by Germaine Copeland

Chapter 4

Wounded Heart

As we continue to talk about our heart, and how important it is to guard it, we have to discuss what role we play in the healing of a heart that is wounded. I wonder how many of you reading this right now are suffering from emotional pain or a wounded heart. *I know I have!* Don't we do a great job covering it up with our fake smiles, and cheerful masks – or all sorts of other business – to avoid the hurt? What games we are good at playing!

We are especially good at playing the roles we create within our family. The people we are closest to have the greatest potential to wound our spirits. These are people we have allowed into our lives, and feel comfortable enough to let our guard down around them. Let me elaborate: when you are leery of someone, you close yourself up. That could mean you are guarding your heart incorrectly. Yet, when you *trust someone,* you open yourself up to them freely. That is why pastors, teachers, doctors, policemen and other commonly-trusted people can be the best people we ever met... *or the worst.* This includes our family members.

Let's start with spouses – a spouse can absolutely be the person in your life who is capable of wounding you the *most* severely. The same is true with kids, parents and grandparents. Some people seem to have a gift for stabbing people where it *really* hurts – just when you let your guard down, that's when they take out their sword and stab you. This is possible because hurt people, *hurt people.* Because so much happens in the family dynamics, and because we are not honest with each other, we begin this painful game of blaming each other. The problem is that we *all* want to be accepted and loved, especially by the ones closest to us. We simply *expect* that when we show love to someone, they will show love *back.* But that's not always true, and when we experience this, we are wounded.

I've seen mothers (including myself) cry over their children who have caused emotional damage by saying or doing things that leave her distraught and wondering where she could have gone so wrong in raising her child. I've also seen children whose emotions are so mixed up, and so hurt, that they are nearly dysfunctional in society. Sometimes it's the parents, or friends, or perhaps another sibling that does something terrible, or continually says something, or does something that makes a child feel so unworthy, so useless and so unloved. I have seen this happen in families, as well: a brother who is wounded within his own heart lashes out at his sister to bring her self-esteem down – saying terrible hurtful things to her – so that he can feel better about himself. Yet in the wake of this, his sister now is left with a wounded heart and feeling a debilitating lack of value. I've also dealt with children and siblings who were so jealous of one another, or of their parent's attention, that it caused a deep division in the family, resentment toward their parents, and the parents were left in shock – wounded and wondering what happened, and where did it go wrong.

A wounded heart is a *spiritual condition*. Let's just say it's a *wounded spirit*, so we can distinguish between the soul and the spirit.

How does one's spirit become wounded?

David speaks about this truth, in

Psalms 55:12-14 "Ahithophel was someone David really trusted, so his betrayal struck deep into David and so to speak smote him under the fifth rib." (KJV)

I know from personal experience that self-hatred causes a deep wound, like a knife stabbed under the ribs, and it has to be pulled out. The healing has to come from *knowing that God loves you with a perfect love.* The Bible says that perfect love cast out fear, but I believe it can cast out *anything.* We need to really understand just how much God loves us, and has forgiven us, and wants so much for His healing power to come and overtake our lives, in order to heal every stabbing wound. We must recognize that self-hatred and offenses that we acquire like wounds are sins, and a weakness of the flesh which will require repentance on our part. Remember, two wrongs never make a right. When we are hurt by someone, we often harbor anger and ill-feelings toward that person. Just as we talked about in chapter three – iniquity is a deep root in our heart that can potentially be handed down from generation to generation. Iniquity is something that usually remains hidden for a long period of time before we recognize the symptoms and then allow the Holy Spirit to pull it out.

Are you aware that our spirit can be wounded just like our physical body can be wounded? If you have ever dealt with a physical wound, you know how it will impact your comfort level, your mobility, your activity level, and many other aspects of your life. Well, a spiritual wound will *also* affect you on so many levels, you may not even be conscious of!

Proverbs-18-14: A man's spirit sustains
him in sickness,
But a crushed spirit who can bear?

Let's spend some time thinking about this, because there are two battles going on within us. When our spirit isn't strong enough to deal with our injury or our sickness, the physical effects can leave us devastated and depleted. The enemy will play on our weaknesses, as we know. So, when our spirit is in a weak condition, we are not going to be prepared for the battle of the physical manifestation when it hits us. When it does come, and we are not spiritually prepared, it can leave us felling hopeless, and even cause us to become discouraged and depressed.

In Proverbs 18:14 in the living bible, we read:
"The human spirit can endure a sick body, but
who can bear it if the spirit is crushed?"(LBV)

Nobody can! So what is God saying to us? We better keep our spirit strong, because we never know when sickness can come upon us.

I have always loved the scripture in the book of James, chapter 1, beginning in verse two:

"Consider it a sheer gift, friends, when tests and challenges come at you from all sides. You know that under pressure, your faith-life is forced into the open and shows its true colors. So don't try to get out of anything prematurely. Let it do its work, so you become mature and well developed, not deficient in any way." (MSG)

I feel this verse is telling us that we should greet a trial as though a best friend just showed up – Wow! That's a hard one to swallow! But as I have grown in my relationship with the Lord, I have come to truly understand that scripture, because he goes on to explain that the trial or *temptation* will reveal the *weak areas of our lives* – only then we can strengthen that area, so that we have no weaknesses. It's such a powerful word, because we don't know where we are weak until a trial comes along, and we see how we respond to it.

I also love the saying, "You can judge a person's spiritual walk by what it takes to devastate them." How are you responding to sickness and wounds of the heart?

Some people can stay strong through very difficult circumstances, and others fall apart at the smallest little problem. You see, God is looking for *maturity* and he will use whatever he can to reveal to us where we need work.

A page from Joan's journal...

Physical Healing

I know very well how debilitating a physical problem can be. Having dealt with bad knees for the past five years, as they got progressively worse, I reached a point where I simply could not do the things I use to do. I began shopping at smaller stores because it hurt so bad to walk the larger supermarkets. Sadly, I had to quit going for my beloved regular walks down the beach, because it was too hard to walk on the sand. I shopped very little, and eventually couldn't do even smaller things, like cook meals and clean my home. It changed everything about who I was. I continued to go to the chapel every day to minister to those in need, and that kept me strong in my spirit.

The scripture says, in Proverbs 17:22 "A cheerful heart is good medicine, but a crushed spirit dries up the bones." (KJV)

We need to keep doing whatever we can to avoid becoming weary in our time of physical disabilities – but if we have a wounded spirit that will be almost impossible to do. The spirit can be said at times to be in a broken, non-working condition. What exactly does that mean? Just like the workings of your physical body – it will cause all sorts of issues in your spirit: Prayer will be difficult, your faith and reliance on God will diminish, your spiritual immune system will be compromised, and you will be subject to spiritual infections – such as unbelief, overbearing temptations – and a host of other spiritual weaknesses will find it easier to take root in you.

We are made up of spirit, soul and body, and they are meant to work in concert for our total health and well-being. The condition of each one will influence how we respond to a trial, or how well we recover from a physical illness.

We read in Psalms 43:5, "Why are you in despair, oh my soul? And why are you disturbed within me? Hope in God, for I shall again praise him, the help of my countenance, and my God." (NASV)

David's spirit was speaking to his soul, and addressing His will. Many times our fleshly *will* invites sin, which can open the doors to our disobedience and rebellion to authority. But a wound to our spirit is something that we have no control over. It is something that hurts us very deeply.

Let me share a true story with you: A father wanted to teach his son that he shouldn't trust anyone blindly. He told his young son to stand on the seat of a dining chair and proceeded to stand in front of the boy with his arms open, and told him to jump to him. Now, as you may know, under normal circumstances, a child will naturally trust its parents. The father continued to call for his son to jump, telling him "You can trust me..." After much coaching, the boy jumped, only to find himself hurt and on the ground with a broken spirit, because his father did not catch him. The father wanted to teach his son that he should not just trust anyone. Such a cruel teaching left his son with a broken and wounded spirit, and a lack of trust, for anyone. This is not a compassionate, let alone effective, way to teach anyone.

A number of years ago, while working with women in our Recovery Home who were struggling to overcome drug and alcohol addiction, those of us running the program used to say, "we have to break their *will*, taking care not to break their *spirit*". So many of these women began using drugs and alcohol as children, to cover up the pain of a broken spirit and a wounded heart. Many times we medicate the *symptom,* and never deal *with the real problem. What made* my heart so heavy, working in this home, was that many of these women struggled so intensely to get to a place where they could even believe that God could love them, forgive them, and heal them. For them, the hurt and the roots of their pain, were so entrenched in their spirits. Many of these women didn't respond to a standard

12-step program for substance abuse — what they really needed was to be held, and loved, and accepted; what they were truly hungry for was the unconditional love they never received from anyone else until then.

How do we overcome our weak spirit?

Trust me, I have asked this question of myself many times in my own life. At times, I was so sick and felt so hopeless that all I could do was turn to the Word, and allow my spirit to rise up and quote scripture, or speak the truth over my life. A few of those scriptures I turned to, and spoke aloud to myself, are here:

> **"If God be for us, than who can be against us?" Roman 8:31(KJV)**

> **"For we know that in all things that God works for the good for those who love Him, who have been called according to his purpose." Romans 8:28 (KJV)**

> **"Be confident of this very thing, that he who began a good work in me will complete it." Philippians 1:6 (KJV)**

"The Lord is with me I will not be afraid."
Psalms 118:6 (KJV)

Reading this aloud in a time of turmoil is called *speaking the truth of God over ourselves.* That is why the Word tells us to speak to ourselves in psalms, hymns, and spiritual songs.

Sometimes, it can be helpful just to lie down and listen to some anointed worship music, or listen to scriptures on tape, especially if you don't feel like reading yourself. David encouraged himself in the Lord, because his spirit was strong. If your spirit is alive and well, you will be able to encourage *yourself* when things go wrong. If your spirit is wounded, you will *discourage* yourself when things go wrong.

If we begin discouraging ourselves when things go wrong, it is like throwing gasoline on the fire. The negative feelings start to bubble up, and when we begin speaking all the wrong things, such as "Why is this happening to me? I never do anything right... I'm just a screw-up... Nothing good ever happens to me... People would be better off if I wasn't around... Why am I even still living? No one cares..." You can see the danger in telling ourselves the wrong story!

We have to come to a place in our lives where we first and foremost **acknowledge** that we have a wound. Because a wound that goes unacknowledged is a wound that cannot be healed. You also can't live in denial of a wound, pretending that it is not there. The reason it is easy to live in denial is because we don't *want* to own it, and be true to ourselves, and therefore we delay our healing. We all have a wounded heart in one way or another, if we have lived in this world for any period of time. We are all living with wounds that need to be healed. Some wounds happen in our childhood, and some later in our lives; they can be inflicted through the course of relationships of all kind: work, marriage and yes – even through the Church body. The hurts that occur within the body of Christ are sometimes the hardest to heal, but for now I want to talk about the wounds of our childhood.

For most of us, childhood wounds tend to stay hidden for many years and then seem to resurface at the most inappropriate times in our lives. One thing is for sure: they *will* come to the surface whether we like it or not, and we get to choose whether or not we will allow the healing process to take place, or just play the "cover up game" for as long as we can.

Many times we think it best to choose to cover up those awful feelings we don't *want* to feel, and we might do just that with alcohol, drugs, and many other unhealthy things – but ultimately they all are a form of denial, and I have seen many times that the results of denial – which we use to protect ourselves – will at some point manifest through our physical body, and cause all kinds of ailments. Strangely, many times that very manifestation can become our comfort, and our way of getting the attention we so badly need.

A page from Joan's journal...
The Manifestation of a Wounded Heart

I want to share the story of my cousin with you. She lived her entire life in denial; she just could not come to terms with the reality that she was sexually abused as a child. She grew up in a family that never talked about anything – a family in denial. There was no safe place to share her pain, so as she entered her 40's with one child and a rocky marriage, she began to look to others to fulfill her needs. This person was very needy, and had no idea what to do with those feelings. The internet had just become a household reality, a place where we could communicate with other people without them really knowing who we are. We could put our feelings out there and not have to reveal the truth of who we were, or where we were coming from. She found a place of safety and acceptance among these strangers on the internet. Because of her need to be heard and to be loved she fabricated an illness, she pretended to have cancer. Everyone felt sorry for her and wanted to hear her story, so she became important and accepted by these hurting people. As time went on, she began to help them with their pain, she could now pretend to be dealing with her cancer and it gave her a sense purpose and a reason to live.

This was her life for several years; it gave her a reason to get up every morning and helped her to overlook the real issue that was going on inside of her. Over time, she became more and more isolated from friends and family. Death became her focus and the afterlife seemed to look better to her than her reality of living. My sweet cousin left this world at the young age of 46, and when she died her death certificate said, cause of death: <u>Unknown</u>. We found out that she never had cancer, yet she did have lot of symptoms, (symptoms had manifested due to her internal pain) but the symptoms were not cancer. Her neediness for attention allowed her to build in her mind all symptoms of cancer and her body followed.

This actually broke my heart to hear this, and to know that our emotional pain can become so overwhelming that we can choose to let go long before our time. What we harbor on the inside will eventually come to the surface, and we get to choose what we do with it. A wound without brokenness and repentance also cannot be healed, because even if someone else hurts you, your feeling toward them must be dealt with, or the freedom and healing will not come. We also cannot justify, or start blaming others for, our wounds and hurts. We can't allow those who caused our pain to control our life through our desire for vengeance, or it will allow them to control your life forever and you'll never be free or healed.

The enemy loves to attack us at the point of our identity. *Do you really even know who you are?* Many of us have allowed our identity to be blinded by our wounded hearts that are speaking louder to us than the voice of God. What happened *to us* does not shape our identity in Christ. It really *damages* our identity, and many of us only see ourselves through our eyes of our brokenness and not through the eyes of our Father who brings wholeness and freedom and a new identity to each of us. God wants us to see ourselves in the light of His fullness that is the righteousness of Jesus Christ.

I realize some of the strongest desires human beings have are to be loved, to be accepted, and to feel that they belong. We want a sense of connection and belonging to something or someone. We want to feel valuable. We cannot be guaranteed of always getting that in our dealing with people, but we **can** get it from God. I know in my life of dealing with a wounded heart I wanted something in me to be filled by my children and grand-children, only to find out that was not happening. Because of my wounds I became needy and began to pull on them with my neediness, only to have them reject me and pull away.

Being needy is so unattractive and really turns others off and away *from you*, not *to you*, as you may so desperately want. We must stand strong now in the truth of who God says who we are. As I began to learn what this statement truly means, and to deal with my wounded heart, God began to show me that what I was wanting from them was something they were incapable of giving to me. I was requiring of them and needing something they could never give me. *WHY?* Because I needed to reach the place of realization within myself that God is the only one who can fill that hole, and being a jealous God, He would never allow someone else to give me, or fill me with, something that was meant to come from Him. So my question to you is: *Do you know what God say's about you? Have you gone to Father God with your wants and needs?* His word is a love letter to you, and He is asking you to run to him and grab hold of His letters and uncover the mysteries and secrets he has for you. It is by knowing God's truth that we are *set free.*

Psalms 109; 22 says, "For I am poor and needy, and my heart is wounded within me." (NASB)

John 8:32 says "You will know the truth and the truth will set you free." (NAVB)

Luke 4:18-19, we read in the message, "He's chosen me to preach the Message of good news to the poor, Sent me to announce pardon to prisoners and recovery of sight to the blind, To set the burdened and battered free, to announce, 'This is God's year to act!'" (MSG)

Sometimes we just need to be reminded of the scripture where **Jesus said, in Matthew 10:29-31, "Not even a sparrow, worth only half a penny, can fall to the ground without your Father knowing it. And the very hairs on your head are all numbered. So don't be afraid; you are more valuable to him than a whole flock of sparrows." (NLT)**

Sometimes just a reminder from God that he knows what I am going through is all I need to keep on keeping on. Just to know that He cares so much even for the birds, and cares even more for me, as his child, can be quite a healing balm for my wounded spirit. You are more valuable to Him than the birds are. You are so valuable that God sent His only Son to die for you. Because God places such value on you, you need never

78

fear personal threats or difficult trials. These things can't shake God's love or dislodge his Spirit from within you.

Do you need healing? Is there a deep-down, painful need in your heart today that no one seems to understand? Has your spirit been wounded and your heart broken and your faith shaken? Then say this prayer:

Father, in the name of Jesus, I come to YOU with a feeling of shame and emotional hurt. I confess my transgressions to YOU (continually unfolding the past till all is told). You are faithful and just to forgive me and cleanse me of all unrighteousness. You are my Hiding Place, and you, Lord, preserve me from trouble. You surround me with songs and shouts of deliverance. I have chosen life. According to your Word, You saw me while I was being formed in my mother's womb; and on the authority of Your Word, I was wonderfully made. Now I am your handiwork, re-created in Christ Jesus.

Father, YOU have delivered me from the spirit of fear, and I shall not be ashamed. Neither shall I be confounded and depressed. You gave me beauty for ashes, the oil of joy for mourning, and the garment of praise for the spirit of heaviness that I might be a tree of righteousness — the planting of the Lord, that you might be glorified. I speak out in psalms, hymns and spiritual songs, offering praise

with my voice and making melody with all my heart to the Lord. Just as David did in I Samuel 30:6, I encourage myself in the Lord.

I believe in God who was raised from the dead, Jesus, Who was betrayed and put to death because of my misdeeds and was raised to secure my acquittal, absolving me from all guilt before God. Father; YOU anointed Jesus and sent Him to bind up and heal my broken heart and liberate me from the shame of my youth and the imperfections of my caretakers. In the Name of Jesus, I choose to forgive all those who have wronged me in any way. You will not leave me without support as I complete the forgiveness process. I take comfort, and am encouraged, and confidently say, 'The Lord is my Helper; I will not be seized with alarm. What can man do to me?'

My spirit is the candle of the Lord, searching all the innermost parts of my being, and the Holy Spirit leads me into all truth. When reality exposes shame and emotional pain, I remember that the sufferings of this present life are not worth being compared with the glory that is about to be revealed to me, and in me, and for me, and conferred on me! The chastisement needful to obtain my peace and well-being was upon Jesus, and with the stripes that wounded Him I was healed and made WHOLE. As Your child, Father, I have a joyful and confident hope of

eternal salvation. This hope will never disappoint, delude or shame me, for God's love has been poured out in my heart through the Holy Spirit, who has been given to me.

In His name I pray, amen.

From: Prayers that Avail Much, by Germaine Copeland

Chapter 5

Strongholds in Your Heart

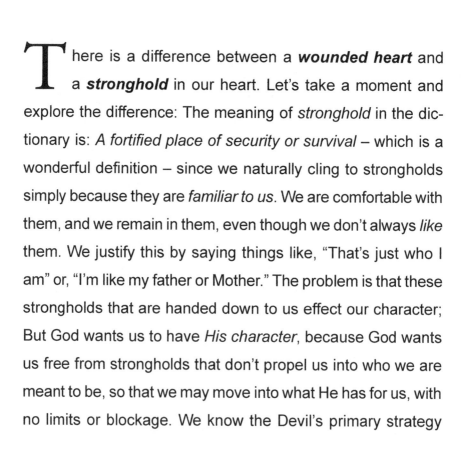

There is a difference between a **wounded heart** and a **stronghold** in our heart. Let's take a moment and explore the difference: The meaning of *stronghold* in the dictionary is: *A fortified place of security or survival* – which is a wonderful definition – since we naturally cling to strongholds simply because they are *familiar to us*. We are comfortable with them, and we remain in them, even though we don't always *like* them. We justify this by saying things like, "That's just who I am" or, "I'm like my father or Mother." The problem is that these strongholds that are handed down to us effect our character; But God wants us to have *His character*, because God wants us free from strongholds that don't propel us into who we are meant to be, so that we may move into what He has for us, with no limits or blockage. We know the Devil's primary strategy is to disguise his activities so that it *appears that someone or something else is to blame.* He wants us to get our attention on his instruments, his hindrances and "wrestle" with them, so that our battle will be directed against the "symptoms" instead of the "real source."

What we mean by a "stronghold in the heart" is really a faulty thinking pattern, based on lies and deception. Deception is one of the primary weapons of the Enemy, because it is the first building block of a foundation for a stronghold. What strongholds can do is cause us to think in ways which block us from God's best for us. I don't know about you, but I'm in a season of my life that I'm wanting *God's best* and not *my own.* It's a good journey to be on!

A page from Joan's journal...
How Strongholds Can Limit You

I once had a huge stronghold in my own heart that had directed much of my life for a very long time, and I never really saw it for what it was until I experienced a profound betrayal. I had worked very hard for many years in ministry, alongside a woman I loved very much, and who I had every reason to believe was my equal partner in building a ministry that we both took on with love and great passion. But, whereas I happily poured my heart into this partnership, I was unaware that my role was actually being viewed by my partner as disposable, and secondary to her role. You see, I was always happy to be helping others in leadership to discover and possess their destinies. And that has nothing to do with them, but everything to do with how I viewed my worthiness to walk into my own ultimate purpose in life.

This stronghold on my life had caused me to believe that I was meant to always stay in the background, holding up someone else's arms. I allowed this stronghold to limit the full realization of my talents, gifts, and abilities. I thought I was meant to remain just an armor-bearer, a supporter of someone else's dream – and there is nothing wrong with that role, except that God had a bigger plan for my life and he needed me to see myself as He saw me. I was always giving so much of myself away, working to fulfill someone else's destiny, that I wasn't leaving any room for my own pursuits. I used to have dreams about driving a car from the passenger's seat, never did I see myself in the driver's seat – this dream illustrated exactly how I saw myself in my waking life. This self-limitation was a huge stronghold that has not been easy to overcome or tear down; it has been a process of going after it, every day for the past 5 years. You see, not until I was abruptly asked to leave that ministry I had spent seven years pouring my heart and soul into, was I able to be shaken in a way that allowed me to recognize the stronghold of self-limitation in my heart. I was devastated by the betrayal of someone I thought viewed me as an equal partner, because I thought my role in this ministry was who I was meant to be, and what I would be doing for the rest of my life.

But as I began to allow God to speak to me about how this could have happened, He assured me that He was in charge of it all, and that it was time for a promotion in my life. He showed me that this devastating betrayal was actually a gift – because it forced me to come face to face with the stronghold I had been caught in. He showed me that it was high-time to use all that I had learned on my journey, to become a pastor myself, a teacher, and an author – which was something I could have never otherwise believed I could become.

The breaking of the stronghold came as I was willing to forgive, to let go of any hurt and anger about the betrayal I experienced, and just trust God with my future. God, in his amazing grace, has restored my faith and taught me to believe in myself. I had never experienced that pain of betrayal, and I pray that I never do again. But what I learned from it all is that God will cause all things to work together for my good, if I will just let Him be in charge. You see, breaking a stronghold is never about what **others** do to **us** in their own brokenness, it is always about what the experience brings out of us. It took that experience for me to recognize my potential and to be willing to take a chance and go for my destiny.

My hope is that sharing the experience of my own painful betrayal, and the way it was a catalyst for great change, will help you see that you don't have to allow something that has a stronghold on you to keep you in bondage any longer! Stop blaming others for the limits you are placing upon yourself; don't feel sorry for yourself, but look inside, and allow you're healing to begin.

One of the most popular and devastating strongholds to have, is an incorrect image in your mind of who God is, and how He sees us. People who see God as a *taskmaster*, live their lives with an unhealthy fear of God. There *is* a good kind of fear of God, which is more accurately described as a *holy respect for Him* — but the Enemy wants us to have a kind of fear where we see God *only* as a taskmaster: cruel, cold, distant, and uncaring; someone who would crack the whip at us the moment we step out of line.

People who find it hard to feel God's love and presence often have this stronghold in the heart. If you feel God is distant and cold, or you question if God really loves you, then you need to get this stronghold torn down. The reason I know this is because I had it for so long. After I gave my heart to Jesus, I began to realize I had trouble seeing God as a loving Father.

As I grew deeper in my walk with the Lord, I began asking myself, and searching my heart, about my image of a loving Father and how it became distorted. I began to realize it was a distortion caused by filtering my view of God through my image of my *earthly Father*, whose love *was* conditional, and to whose expectations I could never measure up. I struggled for many years, wanting His approval not realizing that my *heavenly* Father approved of me from day one! This need within me kept me from experiencing the freedom of true, unconditional love. When you have this stronghold in you, it will motivate you to become a worker bee, trying all the time to be good enough for His approval — never realizing it was never about *doing,* but was always about *being.* This kept me at a distance from God and was a real hindrance in my relationship and intimacy in experiencing the Love of the Father.

A page from Judy's journal...
He Loved Me First

I didn't realize how hard it was for me to feel God's love until one day when I was coming home from a meeting with my prayer partner, and I was listening to a short devotional from Beth Moore. She was telling a story about coming home from a speaking engagement, very tired, and riding in a cab that was approaching her neighborhood. She saw a rays of light shining down on the block where her house was. Of course it was shining down on the whole block. As she looked at the rays of light, she began thanking the Lord for His Love and compassion for her. By the time she got into her home she was filled with love for the Father. She found herself saying over and over again, "I Love you Lord, I love you Lord..." When she heard the Lord share with her, "You know you couldn't say that unless I loved you first. Your response should be 'I Love You too.'" When I heard that, I began to cry uncontrollably, because that really hit my spirit – the notion that when I felt that deep sense of compassion for the Lord, it was because He was loving me first. Something broke that day in me, and that wall – that stronghold – was broken, and a new relation-ship between myself and the Lord opened up.

God made provision through Jesus for us to be holy, blame-less, and set apart for Him. We can live before Him in love without reproach. That means we do not have to feel guilty or bad about all of our weaknesses and faults. I encourage you to *relax* in the Fathers love. Learn to *receive* the Father's love. Think about it, thank Him for it, and watch for the manifesta-tion of it in your daily life. God shows His love for us in many ways, but we are often unaware of it. He loves us first, so we can love Him and other people. God never expects us to give away something that He has not first given to us. His love is poured into our hearts by the Holy Spirit and He wants us to live out the results of it before Him, in love. *Let love in... and let it out.* Take a moment. Take a deep breath, and just breathe in His unconditional Love. Read God's love letter to you, like in

Isaiah 43:4, "You are precious to me. You are honored, and I Love you." (NLT)

Also, the Word reminds you, in Psalms 36:7-9 "How precious is your unfailing love, O God! All humanity finds shelter in the shadow of your wings. You feed them from the abundance of your own house, letting them drink from your rivers of delight. For you are the fountain of life, the light by which we see." (NLT)

You are the apple of His eye and nothing you have done, or will ever do, will change that.

Don't let the allure of staying put within a familiar stronghold keep you from receiving God's Grace, because Grace is getting what we don't deserve. I know in my natural mind I could not comprehend that. Understanding God's Grace was a struggle for me. Being raised in a Catholic Church from a young age and not knowing who God really was, I was never taught Grace. So, to break the strongholds of religion that had been built within me, and replace them with Grace, I had to tear down the *wrong* altars and images that were built in me from a young age and begin again to build a new relationship, a new foundation, and a new altar of Grace with my Heavenly Father.

The word "stronghold" appears only once in the New Testament

2 Corinthians 10:4-5 reads, "The weapons we fight with are not the weapons of the world. On the contrary, they have divine power to demolish strongholds. We demolish arguments and every pretension that sets itself up against the knowledge of God, and we take captive every thought to make it obedient to Christ." (NIV)

The Greek origin of the word "stronghold" means a "fortification such as a castle." In this passage, we are being instructed on how to fight against and "destroy arguments and every lofty opinion raised against the knowledge of God" (verse 5). They do this, not by using the weapons of the world, but by "divine power." We as God's Children must be aware that God has equipped us to overcome strongholds. The Apostle Paul said that "the weapons of our warfare are not carnal (of a fleshly or earthly nature), but mighty in God for pulling down strongholds."

Strongholds in the Heart are birthed from, and dwell in, deception — which are lies and false beliefs. So, naturally the cure for them is to bring the truth in God's Word on the scene. You fight the lies of the enemy, with the truth, which is in the Word of God! You have to get into the Word for yourself, and ask the Holy Spirit to show you the places where you have embraced wrong beliefs and lies, and been deceived from wrong teaching and belief systems that have been established, perhaps even in your own family lineage. This is why it is so important to know *for yourself* what you believe and *how to back it up in the Word.* There are a lot of teachings out there in the world, but not all that we learn from our fellow man is straight from our Heavenly Father.

In John 8:31-36, Jesus tells us that we can be held in bondage due to strongholds in our lives. And His solution was to, "continue in my word... and you shall know the truth, and the truth shall make you free." (v. 32-32) (NIV)

Strongholds are torn down as we meditate on God's Word, which is Truth!

We need to stand firm and know that we are in a battle — and it's a fight to the finish.

In Ephesians 6:10-18, Paul describes the resources that God makes available to His children — the armor of God. Read what it says to us in the Message Bible: "God is strong, and he wants you strong. So take everything the Father has set out for you, well-made weapons of the best materials. And put them to use so you will be able to stand up to everything the Devil throws your way. This is no afternoon athletic contest that we'll walk away from and forget about in a couple of hours. This is for keeps, a life-or-death fight to the finish against the Devil and all his angels.

Be prepared. You're up against far more than you can handle on your own. Take all the help you can get, every weapon God has issued, so that when it's all over but the shouting you'll still be on your feet. Truth, righteousness,

peace, faith, and salvation are more than words. Learn how to apply them. You'll need them throughout your life. God's Word is an indispensable weapon. In the same way, prayer is essential in this ongoing warfare. Pray hard and long. Pray for your brothers and sisters. Keep your eyes open. Keep each other's spirits up so that no one falls behind or drops out. God gives this for us to guard our hearts our minds and our body. The Word says in here we are told how, in an attitude of humility and dependence, we are to avail ourselves of God's resources. Note that we are to be strong "in the Lord" and "in the power of His might."

In this passage we are being assured that God's mighty weapons – prayer, faith, hope, love, God's Word, the Holy Spirit and praise – are powerful and effective. These break down the walls that keep us from getting close to our Father. Even our thoughts must be submitted to His control as we live for Him. Spirit-empowered believers must capture every thought and yield it to Christ, because unhealthy thoughts can take you captive. Instead, as we focus on the resources and weapons of spiritual strength, we can see God give us *specific* and *real* victory. We have dedicated much of this chapter to the strongholds of the Enemy, but let's not forget that the Lord also wants us to *develop strongholds, in Him*. This is where our strength and power comes from. As we break off these ungodly holds on our lives, we will begin to have victory in our daily walk.

In Nehemiah chapter 8, verse 10 (LB), Ezra spoke to the people and said, "Be not grieved and depressed, for the joy of the Lord is your strength and stronghold."

God wants us to have joy in our lives and to be happy, but to do that we must *actively pursue joy*. If we will purposely cultivate a giving heart, and desire each day to be a blessing, we will begin to see things change in our life. The enemy always wants us to focus on what is missing in our life, rather than rejoice over what we are blessed with. As we have shared in this chapter about strongholds, we know that many of them were handed down through generations, and still others were developed over years of pain and hurt in our life. But the **stronghold of joy** has to be *consciously constructed*, and we will surly need to fight for it! It's easy to find things to worry about – but if we could even just learn to laugh a little more, our load would be lighter. Stronghold were given from the Lord for our benefit and for us to put on like; peace, love, joy, kindness, self-control and gentleness, patience. Yet the enemy comes and counterfeits these stronghold with such things as: anxiety, hatred, sadness, bitterness, Rebellion, harshness, impatience.

I challenge you to start off your morning by focusing on your heavenly Father and all that he has done for you in the past and praise Him for all that he is about to do. We have to call forth the things that we need in this life that will take us to the next level with God. I encourage you to go after joy with all you have, and remember the enemy is not as interested in getting your *stuff* as he is your *joy*, because when he gets your joy, he gets your strength.

Chapter 6

A Hardened Heart

Just as there are many diseases and disorders that can affect the physical heart, there are many ailments of the *spiritual heart* that can impair growth and development as a believer. Such as Atherosclerosis, a hardening of the arteries due to accumulated cholesterol plaques and scarring in the artery walls. If this occurs, we are advised to watch our cholesterol levels to help us be aware of any on coming dangers to our arteries. There are parallels between what can happen to us in the physical realm, and what can happen to us in the spiritual realm. Hardening of our *spiritual heart* can also occur – especially since Christ talks about the heart as the hub of human personality, producing the things we would ordinarily ascribe to the mind. For example, scripture informs us that grief, desires, joy, understanding, thoughts and reasoning and, most importantly, faith and belief, are all products of the heart. Jesus tells us that the heart is a repository for good and evil and that what comes out of our mouth – good or bad- begins first in the heart.

I have always related a hardened heart only to the story found in

Exodus 4:22, where the Lord says to Moses, "When you go back to Egypt, see that you do before Pharaoh all the miracles that I have put in your power. But I will harden his heart, so that he will not let the people go." (NLT)

Although Egypt was stricken with one calamity after another when Pharaoh refused to release the Israelites from their bondage, he hardened his heart with pride against the truth that God Almighty intended to deliver His people from Egypt. In Psalm 95:7-8, King David pleaded with his people not to harden their hearts in rebellion against God as they did in the wilderness. There are many things that can harden the heart and lead a person to deny God, and just like cholesterol blocks the blood's flow, hardening one's heart keeps a believer from having a free flow of God's peace and blessings derived from following in obedience.

Guarding against a rebellious spirit and cultivating a spirit of submissive obedience to God's word, therefore, is the first step in guarding the heart against hardening. I used to think people with "hard hearts" were God-haters or, at the least, people in rebellion to Him. That's what I used to think, until one day while reading the gospel of Mark, God began to show me that *I* have had a heart that was at one time hardened. Anyone's heart can be hardened, even faithful Christians.

Hardening of the heart presents itself when we are con-fronted with God's truth, and refuse *to acknowledge or accept it.* The disciples in that scripture didn't want to believe, perhaps because they couldn't accept the fact that this human named Jesus was really the Son of God. *Don't we as well struggle with that fact from time to time – believing that our Father is all powerful and can do all things?* Maybe they dared not believe that the Messiah would choose *them* as His followers – it was too good to be true. I know I struggle with that concept at times when I see the mighty hand of God working through me. Struggling with disbelief happens to all of us. But I realized that the lesson of the disciples having just seen the incredible mir-acle of Jesus feeding over five thousand with next to nothing, yet when away from Jesus presence, forgetting the power of what God was showing them He was able to do, is that we all do this in some form in our own lives. When I got that concept into my spirit, my eyes filled with tears as I realized I have done the same thing in *my* life. My Father has done so much for me on a daily basis, and my job is to recognize, receive, and apply it to my heart — not just in my head.

When we begin to recognize on a day-to-day basis the power of God in our lives, we should be filled with faith, power, and assurance of the God whom we serve. We will begin to **trust** in whom we serve. This trust will grow in us, and will allow us to be able to face any situation that comes our way. In time, our own faulty reasoning won't automatically take over, but our *faith in whom we serve* will instead take over. This opens the door to peace in the midst of a storm, giving us confidence when our finances aren't coming together, and joy when everything around us is in chaos. When we are unable to believe that Jesus our Father is able to handle any situation that comes into our life, we are doing the same thing that the disciples did. They were shocked, amazed, and surprised at the miracle of God walking on water, and I think it's because we all tend to put God in a box, not readily expanding our thinking to include the truth that God **can do all things**. This resistance – this limiting of God with our thinking – is a form of a hardened heart.

The dictionary defines "hardened" as cold, insensitive, unfeeling, and unyielding. Personally, I had to be brutally honest with myself to realize that there were certain areas of my life where I struggled with a hard heart toward God. I had disbelief, I had trust issues, and I had to give these issues over to my Father and start rebuilding our relationship again on solid ground. I either had to ask myself "Do I truly believe He is able, or don't I?" That is what it means to search your heart and begin to be true to yourself.

God made us with the capability to harden our hearts and literally shut out unwanted influences. It was meant to be a positive thing, but because we haven't understood this, what God instilled in us for good reasons has actually worked against us.

In Exodus, Pharaoh is one of the best examples of hardheartedness. His situation allowed pride to overtake his heart and to harden it. The" pride" of your heart will deceive you — you may say to yourself, "Who can bring me down to the ground?" "I will bring you down, declares the Lord" (Obadiah3). Because of his pride and arrogance, Pharaoh's hardened heart dulled his internal ability to perceive and understand truth, which caused him to deny the sovereignty of the one, true God.

We must ask ourselves these five questions that are descriptive characteristic systems of a hard heart: "Am I...?"

...Unable to perceive?

...Unable to understand?

...Unable to see?

...Unable to hear?

...Unable to remember?

These are all questions pertaining to inabilities in the *spiritual realm*. You perceive it, try to understand it, you can see it, you hear it, but you're unable to get a hold of it in your heart. You have knowledge, which is in your head, but not in your heart. So it doesn't stay with you, you're unable to remember. The danger of that is that you can't apply what you've learned to your daily life. It's in the *application* that change comes in our walk. We are called not to just be *listeners* but to be *doers* of the Word. I came across a story recently that I thought spoke very loudly to me about how deception *deafens our ears* and *hardens the heart* when we become familiar with a sound or a smell — something that is offensive to us in the beginning, after a while, we begin to not even notice it is there. It can be insidious, and gradual, and if we don't guard our hearts against this kind of deception, we can find ourselves very confused and hurting – caught by surprise. Here is the story I recently heard:

"A man rented a room directly beside a train track without realizing its proximity. The first night the train came through blowing its horn and almost gave him a heart attack! But after the first few nights, he started getting used to it and would wake up for a few minutes when the horn would blow, and then go right back to sleep. After staying a while longer in this room, he didn't even wake up at all when the train went by. He had hardened his heart to the cacophonous train and its whistle blowing — to the degree that he couldn't even hear it anymore."

The same hardening process occurs within us when God speaks to our hearts and we don't respond. Eventually we stop hearing His voice because our hearts have become hard, and our spiritual perception has been dulled.

Now, hearts can also become hardened when we suffer setbacks and disappointments in life.

Look with me at Matthew 11 -1-3, "The scripture says that when Jesus had finished giving instructions to His twelve disciples, He left and went to teach and preach in the city. But when John, who was in prison heard of the works that Jesus was doing, he sent his disciples to ask 'Are you the one we have been expecting, or should we look for someone else?'" Jesus said to them, "Go and tell John what you hear and see, the blind receive sight, the lame walk, the deaf hear and the dead are raised. And blessed is he who keeps from stumbling over me." (NIV)

We know from scripture that John had walked with Jesus and witnessed His miracles and he knew that Jesus was the son of God, but because – for whatever reason – Jesus did not visit John in prison, and did not *seem* to be concerned about what John was going through, John began to question who Christ was. I don't think John was any different than we are today. Even after we have witnessed the power of God in our lives, and experienced His miracles, we can become disappointed in Him when we go through a terrible trial and He doesn't do what we are *expecting* Him to do. This is why Jesus warned us to not stumble over what we don't understand, or allow ourselves to become disappointed, because often we *don't* understand what God is doing in our lives, or the lives of those we are praying for. But this I **do** know: He is working all things together *for our good*, and don't forget – we are walking out *His* plan for our lives, not *ours*! So, we really need to make sure that we don't allow what we are going through to override what we know to be the truth. When we allow that to happen, we will begin to harden our hearts – and that is a very dangerous place to be.

Our hearts are to stay pliable before the Lord, and I have learned from my own experience that when we do become disappointed in God, we put up a wall around our spiritual self and we will not feel His presence, or see our prayers answered. If you believe that you have become disappointed in God, you just need to repent and ask Him to forgive you, and you will begin to walk with a *new freedom*. You see, no one is immune to trails or disappointment while here on this earth. Yet, just as steel is forged by a blacksmith's hammer, so too can our faith be strengthened by the trials we encounter in the valleys of life. Just remember that God can heal any undesirable condition of the heart. First, we have to recognize the effect that this spiritual disease has on us, and God will help us to know how to remedy our heart's condition when we ask Him: "Search me, O God, and know my heart... see if there is any offensive way in me, and lead in me, and lead me in the way everlasting." It wasn't sin that caused the disciples hearts to become hard – it was their focus on things *other than the miracle* Jesus had just performed. They were understandably occupied with trying to save their lives in the midst of the storm. That wasn't sin. They simply forgot what Jesus was able to do, and they didn't for a moment expect him to be walking on water. Basically, they limited His power by their own limited thinking. When we do that, we pray,

in **Psalms 139:23-24: "Search me, God, and know my heart, test me and know my anxious thoughts. See if there is any offensive way in me, and lead me in the way everlasting." (NIV)**

Let's just confess and repent that we've *been* there – but we are not to *stay* there. After repenting, hard hearts begin to be cured when we study God's Word. Why is this? We are to hide God's Word within our hearts so that we may not sin against our Lord.

Psalms 119:10-11: "I seek you with all my heart, do not let me stray from your commands. I have hidden your word in my heart that I might not sin against you." (NIV)

If we are to live life to the fullest – as God intends – we need to study and obey God's written Word, which not only keeps a heart soft and pure, but allows us to be *blessed* in whatever we do!

Chapter 7

Guarding Your Mind

Everything we do and say begins first with what we are *thinking*. There is an oft-used phrase: "It's all in your mind" – this saying is so very true. The media, society, our friends and family members all influence what we think. For this reason, it is important to learn how to *guard your mind*. Your mind is not only a terrible thing to waste but it is an incredibly useful tool when you learn to use it with care. Every thought and aspiration we ever have starts in our mind. When we allow negative images and thoughts to ruminate in our mind, we will eventually act on these thoughts. However, you don't have to allow your mind to be controlled by negative thoughts and images that will inevitably crop up. Here we will share four ways to guard your mind, using Biblical scriptures.

First, *understand what your mind is capable of.* The same way you can unintentionally ruminate on negative things, you can *intentionally* dwell on positive things! Your mind is capable of renewing.

Romans 12:2 (NIV) says, "Do not conform to the pattern of this world, but be transformed by the renewing of your mind. Then you will be able to test and approve what God's will is his good, pleasing and perfect will."

You can begin renewing your mind at *any* time on *any* day. The dictionary defines "renew" as: "to begin and take up again; to revive; to reestablish; to recover; to restore to a former state; make new, or as if new again." All of these things describe what your mind is capable of achieving when you make the decision to renew it.

Secondly, in order to guard your mind you have to identify *what* you are thinking about and *why*. For instance, did someone hurt you and all you can think about is how to get revenge?

Philippians 4:8 (KJV) says "Finally, brethren, whatsoever things are true, whatsoever things are honest, whatsoever things are

just, whatsoever things are pure, whatso-
ever things are lovely, whatsoever things are
of good report; if there be any virtue, and if
there be any praise, think on these things."

Your mind is not there for you to think about the bad, the negative or the evil, it's for you to think about what's good. Every time you find yourself thinking about something bad, mediate on Philippians 4:8 and remind yourself what you *should* be thinking about. Moreover, remember the more you think on what's bad and evil you will eventually increase the chances that you act on these thoughts.

Our thoughts determine our actions, our moods, our self-image and the words we speak. This is why it is so important that we fight against thinking negative thoughts, because positive thinking helps us to live a positive life! Messed-up thinking results in messed-up lives! You can't think thoughts of defeat and failure and expect to live in victory!

Proverbs 23:7: "For as he thinks in his heart,
so is he." (KJV)

Many Christians allow themselves to indulge in impure thoughts—truly there is a battle going on inside our minds. Let's take a moment to examine what we are thinking about. Just take a minute. Where are your thoughts going right now? Are they lifting you up, or are they tearing you down? Are they drawing you *toward* your heavenly Father, or are they causing you to doubt that He is able?

We don't have to always just accept and continue each thought that comes to our minds. We are all given the ability to choose what we give passage to in our thoughts. It took me a long time to realize I didn't have to allow my *thoughts* to control *me*. Sometimes I would wake up in the morning and have thoughts of insecurity and a sense of loneliness, and even thoughts of abandonment. These thoughts that came over me confused me; I didn't understand how these thoughts could grip my mind so effectively and alter my entire perspective towards myself. After days of struggling and fighting depression I realized that the enemy was planting seeds of insecurity in my thoughts before I even had a chance to renew my mind with the living Word of God. Once I would get into the Word and read what my Father says about me, then I was equipped to take these thoughts captive and renew my mind. Now, when I awaken with such thoughts, I go directly to the Word and give the negative thoughts no place to settle in my mind. Previously, if I dwelled on them for even a short period of time, they had the power to set the tone for my mood for the entire day and would effectively rob me of what the Lord had for me that day.

We must be alert and replace the negative thoughts as **soon** as they come in, with pure thoughts.

II Corinthians 10:5 reads: "Casting down imaginations and every high thing that exalted itself against the knowledge of God, and bringing into captivity every thought to the obedience of Christ." (NKJV)

Here's a word of caution: in the nighttime, when you are ready to shut down and rest, is an opportune time when the enemy loves to come and magnify your problems. Have you ever realized that everything seems worse in the night hours? This is when thoughts and worries about your kids, your finances, your marriage, your job seem to find a space to come to the surface in your mind, and can grip you. This is, therefore, a great time of day to begin to develop the habit of reading a Psalm or Proverb or watching something positive or uplifting on television. Unsurprisingly, it is *not* a good time to go watch the unsettling news of our world, or a murder mystery, or even spend "downtime" taking in all of the chaotic input from Facebook or other social media. What we put in our minds just before we sleep will affect our dreams and even how we wake up in the morning. *God wants us to guard our minds.*

That means we have to call upon His wisdom when deciding what we will and will not allow to enter our minds

On that note...

Many times I have found myself thinking about something that was not good. I have latterly out loud told myself to shut-up. Because we have allowed our minds to control us, I know it is not easy it is something I have to work at because I know when I allow my mind to be in control it never bears good fruit.

Remember, millions of Christians wrestle with negative thinking, we need *not* be overcome by that, *we are overcomers already!* If the Enemy tells you you'll never become anything due to your background, your parents, your lifestyle, your culture, or any other earthly limitations – let me tell you that God is not limited by what family you came from, your education, your social standing, or your race color or creed. ***Our God is able!***

What limits God is *our lack of Faith* – it's our own wrong-thinking again. The Devil says "You don't have what it takes..." ***The Lord says, resoundingly, "Yes, you do!" The*** Devil says "You're not able to..." ***The Word of God says, "You can do all things through Christ my Son who strengthens you."*** The devil says "You'll never get out of debt..." ***God says, "You're going to lend not borrow."*** The Devil says "You'll never get well..." ***God says, "By the stripes on my Son, you are***

healed." The Devil says, "You'll never amount to anything..." ***God assures us, "You are more than a conquer!"***

Thirdly, we need Colossians 3:2 (NIV) which says, "Set your minds on things above, not on earthly things."

It's time to learn how to set your mind on things that are *above*. For example, when you hear someone say something negative about someone and you don't believe it, in your mind you've already (immediately) made the decision that you won't believe what gossip you have heard–that's setting your mind.

Romans 8:5 (NIV) says "Those who live according to the flesh have their minds set on what the flesh desires; but those who live in accordance with the Spirit have their minds set on what the Spirit desires."

To set your mind on what the Spirit desires, you have to also know what the fruits of the Spirit are,

Galatians 5:22-23 (NIV) "But the fruit of the Spirit is love, joy, peace, forbearance, kindness, goodness, faithfulness, gentleness

and self-control. Against such things there is no law."

You can *set your mind* on love, joy and peace. You don't have to set your mind on earthly things, such as lust or greed for material gain and temporary pleasures.

Lastly, the ultimate goal is to have the mind of Christ. How would you achieve this? The above steps are a few good ways to start.

Mark 8:33 (NKJV) reads: "But when He had turned around and looked at His disciples, He rebuked Peter, saying, "Get behind Me, Satan! For you are not mindful of the things of God, but the things of men."

Jesus had to rebuke Peter, because Peter was busy minding the things of *this world* and not the *things of God*. Many of us find ourselves doing exactly what Peter did. We get so consumed by the world and its troubles that we forget we are meant to live *in* the world not *of* this world. We are to have the mind of Christ, and that means we have to be mindful of the things of God.

Philippians 2:2-5 (NIV) gives us a view of this: "Then make my joy complete by being like-minded, having the same love, being one in spirit and of one mind. Do nothing out of selfish ambition or vain conceit. Rather, in humility value others above yourselves, not looking to your own interests but each of you to the interests of the others."

In your relationships with one another, have the same mindset as Christ Jesus. Reading your Bible will also help you accomplish this ultimate goal. God has called us to live *specific* lives, and in order to do so we must also have His mindset.

Every time you get distracted with negative thoughts and images, just remember the ultimate goal: is **a Christ-like mind**. Jesus never worried about what the world was doing; He always stayed focused on His ultimate goal: dying on the cross for our sins. So begin today the practice of *guarding your mind* against Satan's lies and attacks. God did not give us a mind to be messed-up with negative thoughts. God desires us to have peace in our minds.

2 Timothy 1:7 (NKJV): "For God has not given us a spirit of fear, but of power and of love and of a sound mind."

Philippians 4:7 reads: "And the peace of God which passed all understanding, shall keep your hearts and minds through Christ Jesus."

We need to count on God's thoughts. When we do He will fill us with faith, hope and victory. What God gives us–will *keep us,* and keep us keeping on.

Isaiah 55:8: "For my thoughts are not your thoughts, neither are your ways my ways, said the LORD. For as the heavens are higher than the earth, so are my ways higher than your ways, and my thoughts than your thoughts." (NIV)

What should our minds be actively doing?

How do we prepare and protect our minds?

We should begin by guarding the *door to our mind.* To make a connection to our modern lives, you can think about the process of guarding our minds as being similar to protecting our personal computers. If our mind is to be ready for Godly action, we must guard it like we secure our computers. To keep our computer safe from attacks, we try to strengthen its defenses. What can be done to ward off computer problems? Install a firewall. A firewall isolates our computer from outside influences like things that come from the Internet. It allows the data that is "safe" to enter and blocks the data deemed "unsafe" from corrupting our computer or infecting it with a virus. It's no different with our mind! We must strengthen our defenses by installing a spiritual firewall to guard our thoughts.

Proverbs 4:23 "Keep thy heart with all diligence; for out of it are the issues of life." (NIV)

Isn't it true that our thoughts dictate the direction of our lives? The greatest battlefield of life is the mind, and we are constantly at war for its control! If we want to live right, we must put up a spiritual firewall and not allow everything that comes our way to affect our thinking. Don't allow ungodly thinking. If we allow wrong thoughts into our minds, it will result in wrong, sinful actions. We must keep our minds clear, uncluttered, pure and right. By being filled with God's Holy Spirit, it is possible to keep the garbage out of our minds. There are very real, human circumstances, impulses and desires that constantly threaten our thinking. *Have we set our mind in order to guard what has been committed to us? Have we shielded our minds by thinking according to the Spirit?*

Here's an allegory I've always loved, and will share with you now to further illustrate the importance of guarding your mind. It's a story about The Eagle and The Rattlesnake: There is a great battle that rages inside every person—one side of us is a soaring Eagle. Everything that Eagle stands for is good and true and beautiful. The Eagle soars high above the clouds; He soars above the valleys and storms of our lives. Even though, on its flight, it dips down into the valleys, the Eagle builds its nest on the mountain tops. The other side of us can be considered the slithering serpent, the Rattlesnake. That crafty, deceitful snake represents the worst aspects of our humanity— the darker side. The snake slithers coyly and preys upon one's downfalls and setbacks. Who wins this great battle in our life? The answer is—whichever one is fed! *Which creature are you feeding with your thoughts—The Eagle, or the Rattlesnake?* Never forget—***What we focus on, we give power to.***

We are only responsible for our own actions – Everyone is on their own journey. Even though we may hear of others' troubles, and feel compassion toward the issues they're grappling with, we cannot allow our minds to feed on that situation and the negative energy that is stirred up when we invest our time in worrying over someone else's choices. When we do give in to this, we're focusing more on the problem than on the solution and we may open ourselves up to feelings of doubt, rejection and insecurity. A mind controlled by this will rob us of the joy of our day. No person or situation has that right, especially if it robs me of my peace, joy and contentment. When we're stuck cycling over negativity that we have no control over, our minds are not turned toward what is good and pure and right. We are definitely standing still at that point and are certainly not in any condition to grow. Too often we allow others, and *their* interpretation of us, to be our evaluating measurement. Our job and position is to go straight to God and allow *Him* to inform us about the situation, and how we are supposed to handle it.

Here's an example in the Word about David found in **I Samuel 27-30.** King David had moved to the land of the Philistines because he knew that King Saul would not chase after him there. So, with six hundred men, their wives and David's family they moved to Gath. David was a mighty warrior and yet the Philistines still did not trust him because He was a man after God's heart. *Don't you know there was jealousy?* One day after a battle when King David and his men returned to their homes in Zigzag, the Amalekites had snuck in and invaded Zigzag. They burned down the entire town and held captive the women and children and carried them away. When David and his men came to the city, and saw it had been burned with fire, and that their wives, their sons, and their daughters had been taken, they lifted up their voices and wept, until they had no more power left to weep. The men were so upset that they blamed David and were talking about stoning him. Now, remember, David was their leader. But in verse

I Samuel 30:6 (NKJV), we read: "But David strengthened himself in the Lord his God. He didn't listen to the voices of the people... he didn't allow what was being said about him affect who he was in the Lord." He knew the only one who could change this situation was the Lord, so he got alone with God and cried out to him. I'm sure He reminded himself of the victories He had seen the Lord do for him. I'm sure he reminded himself that God is able to change any problem. The story ends with God helping David recover all that was taken from him, because He did not allow His mind to wander and begin to feel sorry for himself – instead He encouraged himself in the Lord.

In order for us to have a great day, we need to have our mind involved in the things of God; we need to be *hearing from God*, and our actions need to be *following God*. That's why God says to allow your mind to be transformed by the hearing of the word. Be alert, be about God's business. The day will play out all on its own. When we're plugged into the right source, we will have the strength needed, which will allow us to feel encouraged and have victory over our day. What we mean by "being transformed" is to change one's thinking and follow another's'. God wants us to follow him. We need to always strive to become more Christ-like, especially in our walk and in the way we love others.

We must first begin to renew our minds concerning God's promises about you being blessed and anointed for increase. I have always said that the biggest battle of all exists within our minds. It's time to repent (change our minds) for believing falsely about God, His provision, and His love for us. Dear believer – we don't have to twist God's arm to bless us! He has already *promised* to bless us, and even made covenant as a guarantee. ***Be blessed!***

From "Prayers that avail much" by Germaine Copeland, we pray this – a prayer for renewing your mind...

Father, in Jesus name, I thank you that I shall prosper and be in health, even as my soul prospers. I have the mind of Christ, the Messiah, and do hold the thoughts (feelings and purposes) of His heart. I trust in you, Lord, with all my heart; I lean not unto my own understanding but in all my ways I acknowledge you, and you shall direct my paths.

Today I submit myself to your word, which exposes and sifts and analyzes and judges the very thoughts and purposes of my heart. (For the weapons of my warfare are not carnal, but mighty through you to the pulling down of strongholds, intimidation, fears, doubts, unbelief and failure). I refute arguments and theories and reasoning and every proud and lofty thing that sets itself up against the (true) knowledge of God; and I lead every thought and purpose away captive into the obedience of Christ the Messiah, the Anointed One.

Today I shall be transformed by the renewing of my mind that I may prove, what is good and acceptable and perfect will of God. Your word, Lord, shall not depart out of my mouth; but I shall meditate on it day and night, that I may observe to do according to all that is written therein: for then I shall make my way prosperous, then I shall have good success.

My thoughts are the thoughts of the diligent which tend only to plenteousness. Therefore I am not anxious about anything, but in everything by prayer and petition, with thanksgiving, I present my requests to God. And the peace of God, which transcends all understanding, will guard my heart and my mind in Christ Jesus.

Today I fix my mind on whatever is true, whatever is worthy of reverence and is honorable and seemly, whatever is just, whatever is pure, whatever is lovely and lovable, whatever is kind and winsome and gracious. If there is any virtue and excellence, if there is anything worthy of praise, I will think on and weigh and take account of these things.

Today I roll my words upon you, Lord – I commit and trust them wholly to you; you will cause my thoughts to become agreeable to your will, and so shall my plans be established and succeed.

In Jesus name I pray, Amen.

Chapter 8

Guarding Your Mouth

Though it may not appear so, there *is* a connection between our tongue and our heart. You will come to resemble and embody what you talk about. Your mouth will do more damage to your heart than anything else.

In **Matthew 15; 16-18** (Max Lucado) Jesus said, **"'do you still not understand? Surely you know that all the food that enters the mouth goes into the stomach and then goes out of the body. But what people say with their mouths comes from the way they think: these are the things that make people unclean.'"**

Today we all work so hard to look great on the outside yet we don't work so hard on what is going on deep down in the heart. It is more important to God what is happening to you and to me on the inside of us. When people become Christians, God makes them different on the inside. He will continue the process of change inside us when we ask for His assistance for change. God wants us to have healthy thoughts and motives, not just healthy bodies. In today's society it is all about the food we eat and how many times we get to the gym. In just the same way that *eating* poorly will affect our health–when we *speak* negatively, it will affect the condition of our heart and the words of our mouth will give us away, because your mouth will have a bearing on your heart.

Proverbs 6:2 says: "you have been trapped by what you said, ensnared by the words of your mouth." (NIV)

James 3:8, "But the tongue can no man tame, it is an unruly evil, full of deadly person " (NIV)

The Word of God says that we should call those things that are not, as *though* they were. In others words we have the power to speak positive words over something, and then see it happen. When we begin to train ourselves to do that, the battle will begin, because the enemy will tell you that you are not speaking the truth. What we have to look at is God's truth and not *our* truth or Man's truth – there is a big difference between all of those. Let me share an example of what I'm talking about, for I *called* myself a righteous woman of God long before I *really was*. Not even realizing that I was calling from my mouth into existence how God was seeing me. God looks at you and me and sees the finished picture. We are wonderfully made in His image and His righteousness, we just have to learn how to walk in all that and it begins with the words that comes out of our mouth.

Many of God's children curse themselves by what they say, not by what they know. I hear all the time young women saying I'm not good enough for God's love, or I'm not pretty enough or smart enough, etc. The fact is we are created in God's image and look just the way He intended us to be. The problem is that the World tells us we are to look a certain way, and be a certain size, and when we don't feel we measure up to that, we often begin to put ourselves down. Then we begin to *speak* negatively, which causes us to come into agreement with the lies of the enemy.

If you have a problem with your tongue – the words you speak – you really have a heart problem. I believe that your tongue will direct where you go, and what you do with your life.

Think about this...

How are you speaking about yourself? Can you look in the mirror and see what God sees in you? Are you ok with that?

How do you speak over your children? Are you calling forth their gifts and talents, or only finding their faults?

How do you speak about your mate? Are you encouraging or discouraging?

It is our job to build one another up. How do you see your job? Is it a blessing or a curse?

Now let's dig a little deeper with this concept; Let me give you an example: after I was saved, I so wanted my husband to find the Lord. The trouble was, instead of *sharing* about the love of the Father, I tried to *scare* him into the kingdom. I left tracts on the toilet roll and tracts in his lunch pail. He wanted to kill me and the God that I served. Then I learned I could begin to call forth His salvation by my words as I prayed for him. I stopped *speaking* God and started *living* God. Yet when he was at work, I prayed over his pillow and bed every day. I would anoint his recliner with oil and bought him a bible and left it on the end table, praying he would begin to desire to read it. It didn't happen overnight but the day came when he began to read it and hunger for more of God. My words were seasoned with grace as I allowed God to do the work in him. Yes, today He serves the Father.

I have watched my husband lose a great job because he could never speak a positive word about the gift God gave him. The consequences of his words had an affect over our entire family. When we curse what God gives us, He will allow it to be taken from us. I understand the reason my husband did that was because of his own insecurities and lack of value and not fully understanding who he was in the Lord. Nevertheless, consequences are the same — he was ungrateful. When we continually put ourselves down, we are limiting God and telling Him with our words that God didn't do a good enough job, or make us right. How sad for Him! We are to be grateful for the air we breathe and the fact that we wake up every morning to a new day. We are to be singing and speaking praises to our Father, for all He's blessed us with.

It would help us a lot more if we would spend more time listening than we do speaking. That's why God gave us two ears and only one mouth. Taming the tongue is not an easy thing to do and cannot be done without Holy Spirit working in our lives. Just being quiet when you want to say something so badly is good training. *Don't we need–at times–some spiritual duct tape?? FYI, it comes in all colors!*

I have found that in Warfare Prayer we can sometimes get so spiritual that we start telling the enemy off and think that He will listen to us or be intimidated by our power, but that is just not true. He is not the least bit afraid of you or me. He only responds to the Word of God. When we are in Warfare Prayer, our best offense against the enemy is the use of the Word of God against him. Jesus was our greatest example when He was tempted by the enemy:

> **James 3:9-12 (NIV) "With tongue we praise our Lord and Father, and with it we curse human beings, who have been made in God's likeness. Out of the same mouth come praise and cursing. My brothers and sister, this should not be. Can both fresh water and salt flow from the same spring? My brothers and sister, can a fig tree bear olives, or a grapevine bear figs? Neither can salt spring produce fresh water."**

Our contradictory speech often puzzles us. At times, our words are right and pleasing to God, but at other times they are violent and destructive. *Which of these speech patterns reflects our true identity?* The tongue gives us a picture of our basic human nature. We were made in God's image, but we have also fallen into sin. God works to change us from the inside out. When the Holy Spirit purifies a heart, he gives to us the ability to use self-control so that our words will be pleasing to God. Our mouth can be a tool that can be used to bring a blessing or a curse — either to ourselves or to someone else. When we allow our mouth to speak what we feel, we open a door that can cause harm to us.

In Deuteronomy 11:26 (NIV) "Behold I set before today a blessing or a curse."

We have a choice over what we say, and we should be silent when we are tempted to allow our unbridled feelings to speak for us. If our heart is still wounded, our words won't be sweet. *Why is this important?*

Look with me at Deuteronomy 30:19 (NIV) "This day I call the heavens and the earth as witnesses against you that I have set before you life and death, blessings and curses. Now choose life, so that you and your children may live. "

This is a verse we need to pay attention to.

Praying is a gift that God gives us to communicate with our Father. When we pray, we must seek God's best for the person we're praying for and God's will for the situation were asking His help in. We need to be careful that we don't begin to tell God what He is to do, or what we are wanting. When we begin to step into telling God how to fix or answer our prayer I call this "witchcraft prayers." This is when we begin to pray what we want to see happen and not God's will for that person or that situation. Our will and desires can get in the way of what we're asking for, even when we believe it is the best for all, we don't have the right to pray for someone to be removed or to leave or to be fired, just because *we feel* it's the best answer to the situation. That is not a Godly prayer and can and will lead you into something that you don't want to be associated with.

If the words you speak surprise you, remember these truths:

- A person with a harsh tongue has an angry heart.
- A person with a negative tongue has a fearful heart.
- A person with an overactive tongue has an unsettled heart.
- A person with a boasting tongue has an insecure heart.

Every part of the body leads us back to the heart. In order to guard our heart, we must pay attention to what we say, and what we listen to, and where we allow ourselves to go.

If you're having trouble with what you say, or how to control your mouth, and you want to grow and repair your heart. Then pray these lines from the book *Prayers That Avail Much* by Germaine Copeland. Pray this each day:

Father; today, I make a commitment to you in the name of Jesus. I turn speaking idle words and foolishly talking things that are contrary to my true desire to myself and toward others. Your Word says that the tongue defiles, that the tongue sets on fire the course of nature, that the tongue is set on fire of hell.

In the name of Jesus, I submit to godly wisdom that I might learn to control my tongue. I am determined that hell will not set my tongue on fire. I renounce, reject and repent of every word that has ever proceeded out of my mouth against you, God, and your operation. I cancel its power and dedicate my mouth to speak excellent and right things. My mouth shall utter truth.

Because I am the righteousness of God in Christ Jesus, I set the course of my life for obedience, for abundance, for wisdom, for health and for joy. Set a guard over my mouth, O Lord, keep watch over the door of my lips. The words of my mouth and my deeds shall show forth your righteousness and your salvation all of my days. I purpose to guard my mouth and my tongue that I might keep myself from calamity.

Father, your words are top priority to me. They are spirit and life. I let the word dwell in me richly in all wisdom. The ability of God is released within me by the words of my mouth and by the word of God. I speak your words out of my mouth. They are alive in me. You are alive and working in me. So, I can boldly say that my words are words of faith, words of power, words of love and words of life. They produce good things in my life and in the lives of others because I choose your words for my lips; I choose your will for my life in Jesus name.

Amen

Chapter 9

Guarding Your Eyes

In the world we live in today, guarding our eyes can be a very hard thing to do. There is perversion of every kind on television, at the movies and even as we walk down the street every day, and it can be hard *not* to look at something that is not good for our soul. We have a terrible epidemic of pornography taking over the lives of many today and causing all kinds of problems in homes and relationships. The problem is that once we have an image in our head, it is very difficult to get it out, and one thing can quickly lead to another.

The Bible says that when the eye is focused clearly on God, the whole body is full of light. But when it is not focused on the right thing, we begin to have issues.

In Matt. 7:3 (NIV) we read "And why worry about a speck in your friend's eye when you have a log in your own?"

This warning comes because we find it easy to see the faults in others and we seem to neglect our own faults. If the focus of our life is on the Lord Jesus, then we will be able to live a life of integrity. But I have learned that is something that we must wholly intend in our hearts to do every day — the distractions are so many. That is why it is so important to start our day in prayer and ask the Lord to order our day and to take him with us everywhere we go. The enemy knows just how and what to use to get us off track.

In order to guard our heart we must focus our eyes on the Lord. *What is before your eyes? Outlook determines outcome!* Abraham was the friend of *God* because he walked by faith and 'looked for a city' whose builder and maker was God. **(Hebrew 11:10).** Lot became a friend of The World because he walked by sight and moved toward the wicked city of Sodom **(Genesis 13:10-12).** Every one of us has some vision or goal before us that determines our value, actions and plans.

We would all do well to imitate David who said, "I will set no wicked thing before my eyes" (Psalms 110:3) (NIV)

The eyes of the soul must be constantly fixed on God's word if we are to be *in* the world but not *of* the world. It is vitally important to be *in the word of God* on a daily basis! We need to meditate on the Word, we need to memorize the Word, and we need to live out the Word in our daily lives. The Word of God gives us guidance for our lives and will help us to discern right from wrong and good from evil.

As in Hebrews 12:2, (NIV) "We do this by keeping our eyes on Jesus, on whom our faith depends from start to finish."

We are to cherish the word of God and even keep our hearts in a submissive place of wanting to obey the Word. It's not enough to just read or listen to the Word of God but we must *want to be obedient* to what it is saying to us.

When the eye is focused clearly on God, the whole body is full of light

Matthew 6:22-23 (MGS) says, "Your eye is a lamp for your body. A pure eye lets sunshine into your soul. But an evil eye shuts out the light and plunges you into darkness. If the light you think you have is really darkness, how deep that darkness will be!"

If the focus of our life is on the Lord God, then a life of integrity can be lived. You'll be true in deed and heart to your spouse, honest in your business dealings, a good worker, a good husband or wife, father or mother. My friend shared with me an old idiom: If a farmer keeps his eyes on a distant object like a fence post while he's plowing, he'll make a straight furrow." If you can plow a straight furrow by keeping your eyes fixed on a distant object, surely the principal should also be true of plowing a straight and righteous life.

This focus only comes from the wisdom you get from the Word of God. The Bible is filled with all the wisdom that can only come from God's Word. The Bible is filled with all the wisdom we need to deal with any situation that might come our way. Proverbs is the *book of wisdom* and there is one for every day in a month, called words to live by. Use them to guide you on your way!

Guarding your eyes is so important because your eyes are truly the windows to your heart. Your eyes are the gateway to what goes into your mind and what enters your thought patterns, and ultimately, your heart. Let me explain what I mean; We fail to realize that what we allow our eyes to see has an effect on us, it also can open doors to the spirit of fear, depression, confusion, doubt and disbelief. What we often neglect to realize is that *once we see it*, it becomes a part of your thought processes, and it's very difficult to un-see something! That vision is now in your mind and can even move to your heart. We innocently open that door by what we talk about, what we watch in movies, video games we play, and television we watch. When taking in these images, we often we become numb and immune to looking at things that are not good for us, or that don't feed the spirit. We become numb to murder, violence and sexual explicitness seen. Watching this over and over again makes it a "normal" part of life; we are not shocked anymore when we see these things — we/re not even affected by it anymore! What wasn't ok last year is now ok now. We once thought it was wrong, now we just look the other way. This is truly an issue of the heart!

The heart in the Word of God is not referring to the organ in our chest; it is referring to our "inner man." It is the center of our mind, our emotions, and our will. It is the very essence of who we are. We know it's important to us – and since Proverbs talks about the heart 90 times, that tells me it is *very* important to God and to our wellbeing. Yet we seem to just take it for granted.

Matthew 13:16 (NIV) "But blessed are your eyes, because they see; and your ears, because they hear."

A page from Joan's journal...

Being honest with myself

I had an experience this week where what I saw with my eyes totally changed how I felt, emotionally and physically. I had to honestly tell someone that I no longer wanted to spend time with them, because the relationship had just become no good any longer, for either of us. This person was upset and disappointed to hear this, and seeing their reaction caused me to change from a smiling state of peace and being fine with myself, to being sick to my stomach and suddenly having thoughts of responsibility for another person's condition. I began feeling that I caused their pain because I no longer was going to hang with them, since I came to realize it simply wasn't good and healthy for me anymore, and I was only being truthful and honest with myself within our relationship, for the first time. I realized that what I saw with my eyes affected my emotions and my heart and the feeling of guilt came over me like a wave. Even though none of us is responsible for another's reaction to our honesty, we often feel that we are. It made me realize that even my eyes have an effect on my heart which rules my feelings. It can jerk us out of the real truth of a moment and pull us into a false reality, leaving us confused and disoriented. None of these feelings are from God, and we need to go back to guarding our eyes. Truth isn't just a relative **feeling,** *and truth has nothing to do with denial. Being honest with our-selves is about truly coming to realize that we are only respon-sible to live and speak truth for* **ourselves** *and* **NO** *one else.*

Chapter 10

Guarding Your Ears

We are, each of us, blessed with ears at birth and most of us are blessed with ears that can hear. What we hear affects what we think. Just the other day I ran into someone I really didn't know very well, myself, but had *heard* some things about her from other people, and because of what I had *heard*, I had already formed an opinion about her. What we hear can have such an effect on our perspective of people. Later that day, I had the chance to talk with this person and to spend some time with her, and I was surprised that she was nothing like I had perceived her to be and especially what I had heard about her. This situation really spoke loudly to me about being careful what I'm listening to, because it can and will cause false judgments about people. I really had to confess that before the Father; for labeling someone I didn't even know.

Hearing things can shape your impressions and ingrain false images in your mind. God is wanting to open doors of freedom to each of us but sometimes that door doesn't open because we have already formed an opinion about someone or something he puts on our path: a church, a pastor, or job, or town. Many times it stops us from trying new things or embracing the new direction that God has for us. Yet we need to be willing to make that move with him. *How do we do that?* First of all, we need to allow ourselves to be *open* only to the things that God is asking of us. Life is so short, and we waste so much time; we miss the bigger opportunity because we listen to everyone but God. We need to be *living on purpose,* knowing His full plan for us and then being willing to do it. *Sounds easy… it's not!* Walking with the Lord takes effort, energy, and a new perspective. Wanting what the Lord wants, takes humility, willpower, and obedience. Not something everyone is willing to do.

Galatians 2:20: (NKJV) "I have been cruci-fied with Christ: it is no longer I who live, but Christ lives in me: and the life which I now live in the flesh I live by faith in the son of God, who loved me and gave himself for me."

Allow yourself to be overwhelmed with the amazing Godhead you are speaking with. Rest in Him; wait on Him;

Listen to Him; reflect on the One who loves you more than you love yourself. You're having a conversation with your Heavenly Father and He wants to speak back to you! The God of the Universe loves you and loves to hear your voice and wants you to have a hunger for Him.

As we read in Romans 5:5 (NKJV) "And hope, does not put us to shame, because God's love has been poured out into our hearts through the Holy Spirit, who has been given to us."

We must hear what the Spirit is saying to us in this verse!

Also in Psalms 143:8-10 (NKJV) "Let the morning bring me word of your unfailing love, for I have put my trust in you. Show me the way I should go, for to you I entrust my life. Rescue me from my enemies, Lord, for I hide myself in you. Teach me to do your will, for you are my God; may your good Spirit lead me on level ground,"

and in Isaiah 54:10 (NKJV) "Though the mountains be shaken and the hills be removed, yet my unfailing love for you will not be shaken

nor my covenant of peace be removed, says
the Lord, who has compassion on you."

Hearing about what God is saying to you and to me is so much more important than anything this world is trying to say to us. We need to be listening to the right voice and not the counterfeit.

We must spend time with Him, and we must meditate on His voice, hearing from His word. His word is living and active and alive, and it is life to us, opening worship to us as we discover His heart and desires. Apart from this kind of lifestyle, it becomes very difficult to know God's will for our lives. For, within the life that is saturated in devotion we will find an ease and flow of knowing His will, if we're open to finding it, and willing to look for it. God wants to speak to us clearly. This clarity will extinguish any doubt that we might have right now – this comes through the power of the Holy Spirit, which is given to each and every one of us so that we may experience a time of intimacy with the father – this insight will instill in us the deep knowledge of His love, the knowledge of His will, and the knowledge of where we are going. (We need to all be hungering for that).

One of the reasons God's people can get into trouble is that, at times, they follow the wrong voice. That means we need to filter our hearing and learn to discern the voice of God from the voices of people around us, and we are meant to learn that through His word. Believers are to listen to, and obey, only to the Good Shepherd, which is Jesus Christ. He alone can meet our needs; He alone can guide us in righteousness; He alone can protect us from evil; and He alone can bless us richly from above. We can trust Him fully because He laid His life down for His sheep. Let me ask you this question:

Do you know the voice of your Father?

What we all need to realize is that humans are a lot more like sheep than we care to admit? In this life, we don't really know where we're going, even when the landscape looks familiar. But The Shepherd has our journey perfectly planned. Our job is to keep within the range of His voice instead of straying into pastures that look green and tasty. Of course, the path before us will not *always* appear safe and easy. **Psalm 23** speaks about the valley of the shadow of death. Furthermore, the trip to the green pastures and still waters that we long for may take much longer than we'd like – the Shepherd, at times, goes the long way around. In other words, His promised provisions frequently do not come in exactly the form or time frame that we anticipate. But as long as we're following His voice, we are right where we should be. Through experience, a sheep learns to identify its master's call. We also learn to discern Jesus' directions by knowing His voice, by reading His words and following His teachings. Then, when another voice tries to lead you astray, we can say, "No! For the Lord is my Shepherd!"

Proverbs 4:20-21 (NLB) reads, "My child, pay attention to what I say; listen carefully to my words. Don't lose sight of them let them penetrate deep into our heart."

Whatever I allow to enter into my ears will have the opportunity to influence my mind, my heart, and my decisions. So, I need to be careful what I'm listening to. To gain wisdom we must be attentive to the Word of God. The Bible says that faith comes by *hearing, and hearing the word of God*. It also teaches that, without faith, it is impossible to please God. We need to be growing in our faith walk with God. Faith is the substance of what we are hoping for – with no evidence. You will never be a man or woman of faith unless you spend time in the word of God. We must speak out loud the Word of God so our ears can hear and allow it into our spirit, especially if we are struggling with something. We are meant to have God's wisdom for our life, for He has the answers to every problem that arises.

How do we begin hearing the Word of God?

We begin hearing the Word of God by training ourselves to read the Word and listen to its instruction; it has to become a habit, something that you are determined to do on a daily basis. We all have natural tendency to not listen, but you must be determined to focus and pay attention. We all need to find what works for us: I love to listen to audio teachings on the Word when I am in my car driving. I think it's because I'm able to really focus and hear what is being taught without any distractions.

Find what works for you, learn to listen more to different teachings, and carve out a time during your day where you feel like what you are listening to is really able to sink in. Learn to recognize and minimize distractions; set aside time just for you and the Lord to talk – really He needs to talk and we need to listen more. The enemy will try every way in the world to distract you from being in the Word, and from hearing what the Lord wants to say to you for that day. Just be prepared – for I know, it's a battle.

Once again, please be on guard for what you listening to. Many people do not realize all the parts of our body make us who we are, so we should be listening to things that brings us peace and joy and make us feel good about ourselves and about life. We have had things spoken over our lives as children that have affected the way we see ourselves and even how we feel about ourselves. Those words spoken over us may have created a poor self-image and have pulled out and replaced what our Father in heaven says about us. This can leave us with the wrong impression of who we really are. I know, personally, my step father told me all the time how stupid I was, and after a while, I really believed I was just a stupid person! It took many years of me speaking to myself and hearing what I was saying to believe the truth of what God said about me and to stop listening to lies that man said about me.

Chapter 11

Guarding Your Feet

Our feet are useful in helping us embody that force that directs us into our future. I remember when my son was only two-and-a-half years old, I had worked very hard to teach him how to walk. Because of his disabilities, this was not an easy task. My husband would hold him up under his arms while I would take his feet and begin to place them one at a time in front of him–step by step–and I remember doing this exercise for *hours* hoping that it would register in his brain. I recall the first time I saw him standing up on his own and picking up his own foot–step by step–and place it down in front of him — tears began to stream down my face as he was finally grasping the concept of walking. I believe this is what God is doing with us. He is teaching us to guard our feet because he knows that another part of your being–that spiritual heart–directs our feet on our path through life.

Proverbs 4:26-27 (NLT) says "Mark out a straight path for your feet; then stick to the path and stay safe. Don't get sidetracked; keep your feet from following evil."

God is warning us here because, in a sense, we vote with our feet. Our Father knows that our feet lead us–very literally– on our way in life; we are warned in this way because our feet can direct us many times to places we have no business going. In other words, we are meant to watch our step if we are to guard our hearts. If we watch the path of our feet–literally and figuratively–then our future will be established.

God wants us to know that He guides our path, if we will allow him. We must watch–and carefully consider–our steps if we are to guard our heart. The Hebrew translation for "watch" or "ponder" translates more accurately as "to weigh" or to "make level." It is from the same root word as "scales." The wisest way to examine a path we want to take is not at the end of our life or even in the middle of the journey, but at the beginning. Our Father says that He will be that light for our feet when we are not sure of where we are going at that moment. He is training each of us to take each step *with Him* and not to follow our flesh. If we will allow His training in where we go and who we follow, we will chose the right path–the Lord's path–and the promise is that all your ways will be established, righteously. Take a look at what activities you are presently a part of and see if you are honoring Christ in them.

> **The Lord says in Jeremiah29:11 (NKJV) "For I know the plans I have for you says the Lord, They are plans for good and not for disaster, to give you a future and a hope."**

Think about this...
Where are you headed right now?
Do you know the plans that God has for you and your future?

Here's an image for you: The Devil was having a yard sale, and all of his tools were for sale there, and marked with different prices. They were shiny and attractive and labeled. There was hatred, jealousy, deceit, lying, and pride–all at expensive prices. But over to the side of the yard, on display, was a tool more obviously worn than any of the other tools. It was also the most costly. The tool was labeled "DISCOURAGEMENT." When questioned, the Devil said, *"It's more useful to me than any other tool. When I can't bring down my victims with any of the rest of these tools, I use discouragement, because so few people realize that it belongs to me."* Satan's is never happier than when he sees people giving in and giving up to despair and becoming lost in hopelessness. Have you ever felt like your whole world is caving in around you, and there is absolutely no hope? Your troubles seem to build and swell until they appear insurmountable! Well, cheer up – I have good news! There **is** hope for the hopeless!

Even in this last year of uncertainty for so many of us, God has given His people great promises to ensure their safety and increase their courage.

Psalm 18:36 (NKJV) reads, "You enlarged my path under me, so my feet did not slip."

God promises to give us a firm foundation in shaky times, and He also promises to make our feet like those of a mountain deer, able to not only stand on this firm foundation but scale the highest heights of the Spirit – above the chaos of this world.

Just because we are existing – walking and talking – does not mean we are truly awake. Amazingly, in spite of all the signs, wonders, and warnings announcing that we are truly in the last days, Jesus said there will also be a mysterious drowsiness that we must discern and overcome, which comes from losing our God-seeking hunger for him. When this slumbering spirit approaches, it first dulls our perception. Soon, our zeal for the things of God diminishes. We still love the Lord, of course, but our vision sits in the back seat as other less important aspects of life set the direction for our lives.

This bring me to our Word for this chapter, and that is: Steps for Our Future".

Psalm 37:23 (NKJ) reads, "The steps of a good man are ordered by the Lord, and He delights in his way. Though we fall, he shall not be utterly cast down; for the Lord upholds him with His hand."

So who *is* this "good man" in whom the Lord delights? The person in whom God delights is *one who follows God*, trusts him, and tries to do His will; seeking, asking and putting Him first in all that we do. We're talking about steps: The word says God *orders my steps*. That tells me that I can rest peacefully with the knowledge that He has things in order. I'm not just wandering aimlessly, but there is a *purpose for my life*, and yours. Who likes steps anyhow? I don't because they hurt my knees! Steps aren't purely ornamental, though we try to make them pretty by adding all kinds of things to them, like carpet or plants and greenery around them, even ornate wood banisters – but the real *purpose* of steps is to take us to a higher level.

In a spiritual sense, taking these steps serve the function of propelling us in our walk of faith to a higher degree of service to God, a purer joy, and a lasting peace.

Yet, sometimes as we take these steps in our lives, it seems like we've been stuck on the same step for a long time — like we're on hold. But don't forget: God's delays are his appointments! That's when I feel I need to help God and start doing. Not realizing that I'm trying to change and override God's steps for me that I'm working toward my own destination not His. We're not supposed to focus on what we're *waiting for* but focus on the *blessings, right where we are.* If you miss Him in the waiting, you'll definitely miss Him in the blessings.

Look at Proverbs 16:9, (NKJV) "A man's heart plans his way, But the Lord directs his steps."

While I'm in the holding process, God has been waiting on me to learn this lesson. Especially if I'm trying to jump over and skip a step that's ahead of where I need to be; this is when we feel like we've scaled the same mountain over and over again. God is saying "Go back, and learn from the step that you've just tried to skip." These steps God orders for us are tools He's using, and these tools are intended to prepare us for His blessings. These are blessings that He has already been holding up for us. He's equipping and teaching us how to handle this blessing, and how to trust his Word and his timing for our lives. Yet, in these times is when we want to run the other direction! Running only prolongs the training and prolongs the outcome.

> **Proverbs 20:24 (NKJV) says, "A man's steps are ordered of the Lord; How then can a man understand his own way?"**

> **Also, in Isaiah 55:4-5 (NKJV), "for my thoughts are not your thoughts neither are your ways my ways, declares the Lord. As the Heavens are higher than the Earth, so are my ways higher than your ways and my thoughts than your thoughts."**

It is during this time of waiting, and growing, that we often become weary in doing good — it is at this time we can get disappointed with God because He's not moving "fast enough." It's at this time we want to lay down fall sleep. Even just sit down and give up! This is when we begin to cry and whine and complain and worry.

That brings me to step two of "Steps for Our Future": The need to press on. Look with me at

Philippians 3:12-14 (NKJV) "Not that I have already attained, or am already perfected: but I press on, that I may lay hold of that for which Christ Jesus has also laid hold of me. Brethren, I do not count myself to have apprehended: but one thing I do, forgetting those things which are behind and reaching forward to those things which are ahead, I press toward the goal for the prize of the upward call of God in Christ Jesus."

We don't have to be on top of the stage to be grateful. We don't have to wait until everything is in order. We need to praise God for where we are *right now*. Because God is not finished with any of us yet — He is calling us to stand with Him in this last hour and this new season that is ahead of us. God wants to fill you with his glory and His fire; He wants to renew your thinking, your spirit, your soul. Yes we're in a battle, but God is trying to teach us how to use the tools He's given us to fight this. Praise is one of these tools. Praise God that you're not the same as you were yesterday! Praise God that He orders your steps, and that means you won't be on this same step for ever. Praise God that you can press on toward His goals for you, and that we all can press on to overcome depressions; press on to overcome loneliness; press on to triumph over fear;

Press on to move beyond any sickness; Press on to overcome discouragement; and press on to conquer the hurt of rejection.

The Devil thinks He has you cornered on this step, but when you start praising God for the step you're on, The Devil loses his grip on you because you're pressing on, despite feeling stuck, and you refuse to give up! Instead of being defeated, you're pressing-on and asking God for new direction, new guidance, new instruction, seeking his kingdom and his will for your life. Pressing-on causes you to get honest with your-self, realizing God is working on your heart issues.

So how do I do this? I wake up in the morning and I press on toward the goal for the prize of the upward call of God for my life. In my car, on my commute to work, I say aloud "I'm reaching for you today, Lord… I'm reaching for your prize and your call." Because when we press on through the debilitating grip of feeling spiritually stuck, it gives us energy — to fight and to move us forward. Our mind and face are set like a flint toward His calling. Let me tell you, we can't have the energy to fight if we're sitting down! Just when the enemy thinks he has you because you're down — get up on your FEET and press on!

Finally, step three of "Steps for Our Future": Forgetting those things which are behind and reaching forward to those things which are ahead. Some of us are living in the thrilling and scary moment of the build-up for the next big change in our lives that will allow us to step into our blessed and fruitful future. Some of us feel very vulnerable in this moment. The Lord shared with me: "Fear Not! I am forming a protection around you at this time. You will be new for the world to see in the days ahead! In the midst of this forming, I am wrapping my wing around you like a cocoon. Do not fear! For in this transition time, I will cover you and bring you forth in a way that will let you will soar in this next season."

As you put a guard over your feet, be assured that your Lord covers you, walks with you, and protects your steps, as He protects your heart. Will you let Him be that light to your path? Let this really take root in your heart:

"The steps of a good man are ordered of the Lord."

Chapter 12

The Promise of Guarding Your Heart

When we are obedient and follow the leadings of our Father, we are blessed with the promises from God for our obedience. God promises to us bring true life to our time here on Earth, and these promises are so important to receiving God's fullness. To live in the full light of all God promises us, we need to learn to guard our hearts, our minds, our eyes, our ears, and feet. Remember, the Word shares with us,

> in **Proverbs 4:22-27 (MSG) "Dear Friend, listen well to my words; tune your ears to my voice. Keep my message in plain view at all times. Concentrate! Learn it by heart! Those who discover these words live really live; body**

and soul, they're bursting with health. Keep vigilant watch over your heart; that's where life starts. Don't talk out of both sides of your mouth; avoid careless banter, white lies, and gossip. Keep your eyes straight ahead: ignore all sideshow distractions. Watch your step, and road will stretch out smooth before you. Look neither right nor left: leave evil in the dust."

God is not only *warning* us, but at the same time in this verse is sharing a life that will be full and with His promises. I love learning about the promises of God, in His Word. God always shares a warning, before he teaches how to receive a blessing. In these teachings He gives us instruction for guarding our hearts, revealing to us the benefits to be found if we choose to follow, and listen, and pay close attention to what is shared with us. God knows that we are living in a day and time when we need to hear what *He* is saying and not what *man* or *this world* are saying. We need to ask ourselves: *What is our job? Do we want the fullness that God has promised us?*

In Romans 12:2, (NKJV) we read, "Do not conform to the pattern of this world, but be transformed by the renewing of your mind.

Then you will be able to test and approve what God's will is—his good, pleasing and perfect will."

We are to receive a heart after God. Colossians 3:1-2 (NKJV) says, "Since, then, you have been raised with Christ, set your hearts on things above, where Christ is, seated at the right hand of God. Set your minds on things above, not on earthly things."

Setting our hearts on "the things above" means we are striving to put Heaven's priorities into daily practice. Setting our minds on "things above" means we are concentrating on the eternal rather than the temporal. To know God shares all this because He wants the best for us, He wants us to walk in righteousness that is in right standing with Christ. Our job is to be an example to this world and to have the blessings of God in our life,

as shared in Psalms 119:1:7 (NKJV) "Happy are people of integrity, who follow the law of the Lord. Happy are those who obey his decrees and search for him with all their hearts. They do not compromise with evil,

and they walk only in his path. You have charged us to keep your commandments carefully. Oh, that my actions would consistently reflect your principles! Then I will not be disgraced when I compare my life with your commands. When I learn your righteous laws, I will thank you by living as I should!"

This verse relays so clearly the promises of God. We are blessed when our ways are blameless and when we walk according to the laws of the Lord. God's precepts are his commandments and his principles, issued with authority; God is telling us that when we learn to guard our hearts we walk in peace and abundant life, which is God's desire for us. We aren't sharing the light when we're being miserable, with anxiety and no peace or rest. When we live like that, we are laying mixed seed. We are meant to be living a life that demonstrates God's love and His righteous laws, as shared in

Psalm 85:10 (MSG) "Unfailing love and truth have met together. Righteousness and peace have kissed."

They kiss each other! Here, the Word is telling of intimacy. Every promise in the word is ours! Let me share that again" every promise in the word is ours! It is a struggle to live life guarding your heart in a healthy way, since our world is drowning in a sea of sexual images and sinful attractions; we are being pulled from what is right into whatever feels good. Watch, and be on guard, that you are not pulled into which is worldly and not Godly. This is why God says "Above all else..." This is the only place in scripture that says "above all else... guard your heart." Our Father knows that our enemy knows just how to pull us in. We need to know the Word, it is so important for us to hide God's Word in our heart, so we may not sin against Him. We make this prayer the truest desire of our day-to-day life: "Lord to teach me your decrees; teach me your laws; teach me your ways; teach me your wisdom; teach me your understanding; teach me your knowledge."

When you begin guarding your heart as God intends for us all to do, you will be amazed at the things that will begin to develop in your life – they will be incredible! The promise of peace without fear, and a life without chaos and confusion – this only comes when "above all else," you *guard your heart.* If you allow Him to, you will begin to see that God is always teaching us how to be aware of, and purposeful in, deciding where we *walk*, what we *think about*, what we *listen to*, and what we allow our *eyes to look upon,* and to be cognizant of the words that come out of our mouths. These heart issues will be addressed and resolved in our spiritual hearts as we surrender control of our lives to God's will. If you'll step out in faith, and with trust, His divine desire will be allowed to work in your life in ways that are greater than you ever imagined, and He will bestow every wonderful blessing His Word has promised, upon your life. Amen!

Scripture Quick-Reference Guide

Galatians 5:22-23

Mark 8:33

Philippians 2:2-5

2 Timothy 1:7

Isaiah 55:8

Proverbs 4:23

1 Samuel 27:30

Chapter 8:

Guarding Your Mouth

Matthew 15:16-18

Proverbs 6:2

James 3:8

James 3:9-12

Deuteronomy 11:26

Deuteronomy 30:19

Chapter 9:

Guarding Your Eyes

Matthew 7:3

Hebrew 11:10

Genesis 13:10-12

Psalms 110:3

Hebrews 12:2

Matthew 6:22-23

Matthew 13:16

Mark 8:18

Chapter 10:

Guarding Your Ears

Galatians 2:20

Romans 5:5

Psalms 143:8-10

Isaiah 54:10

Psalms 23

Proverbs 4:20-21

Chapter 11:

Guarding Your Feet

Proverbs 4:26-27

Jeremiah 29:11

Psalms 18:36

Psalms 37:23

Proverbs 16:9

Proverbs 20:24

Philippians 3:12-14

Chapter 12:

The Promise of

Guarding Your Heart

Proverbs 4:22-27

Romans 12:2

Colossians 3:1-2

Psalms 119:1-7

Psalms 85:10

CPSIA information can be obtained
at www.ICGtesting.com
Printed in the USA
FSOW03n0802040515
6873FS

9 781498 416702